PRAISE FOR *ABINA AND THE IMPORTANT MEN*

"*Abina and the Important Men* makes a signal contribution to the teaching and learning of history by engaging students at multiple levels. The use of graphic representations and a compelling character-driven narrative succeeds in immersing students in a foreign time and place, and in doing so restores voice to a woman whose story would otherwise have been lost to history."

KENNETH R. CURTIS, *California State University, Long Beach*

"*Abina and the Important Men* stands alone. It is neither a textbook nor a primary source reader, because unlike those types, it offers a discrete, contained, contextualized, and concentrated discussion/analysis of a single primary source, a remarkable document that serves naturally as a bridge to an equally remarkable discussion for students of what it means to "do" history, and to think and write historically. Thus, by so creatively contextualizing a historical corner of Africa, it is both a fantastic introduction to African history and an illuminating introduction to the cognitive challenges and benefits of historical thinking. Whereas standard textbooks are typically information driven and beholden to content coverage requirements, *Abina* offers the great luxury of narrating and investigating a dramatic moment in time. It invites and encourages much thoughtful consideration and discussion with students—with *Abina*, we're not just hurrying off to the next multiple-choice question, but investing in real problem solving."

CHRIS PADGETT, *American River College*

"*Abina and the Important Men* is, without question, the best and most accessible introduction to historical thinking that I have encountered. Students are engrossed by the story and the illustrations; it excites them in ways that no other text has. It obviously tells an important story about slavery and colonialism in nineteenth-century Africa, of great use to any course that touches on these subjects. But, it's greatest contribution to the classroom is conveying to students, through Trevor Getz's encounter with Abina, what historians do and why our work is important. Reading this text makes students understand that history is more than a set of facts and dates; removing this mental barrier opens up new possibilities for engaging them in the excitement and value of studying the past."

CHARLES V. REED, *Elizabeth City State College*

"The quality of the illustrations in this text makes the life history of Abina Mansah more accessible to undergraduates with little experience in African history or the history of slaves. Additionally, by providing the court transcript in the book, this text enables professors to address the difficulties of methodologies and recreating historical contexts with piecemeal empirical evidence."

SARAH ZIMMERMAN, *Western Washington University*

"Abina's heroic efforts to gain her freedom and her moving trial provide a strong narrative that engages students in the young woman's struggle against the rich and powerful men who seek to control her. Getz's is a talented historian who does a wonderful job contextualizing the story. The book also provides readers with the transcript of the case which allows them to understand the difference between primary and secondary sources and the other teaching tools are equally useful and raise important questions for readers to consider."

RANDY SPARKS, *Tulane University*

"This text brings African history to life. By presenting a compelling historical saga in graphic form, the authors help readers to think critically about the institutions of slavery and what it meant to be "enslaved" as a woman during the 18th century. My students love reading this book, and read it from cover to cover, which enables us to discuss Abina as a historical subject, as well as the ways in which history is constructed, contested, and revised."

ALICIA C. DECKER, *Penn State University*

"*Abina* is an outstanding introductory text for my course. For students who are wary of the academic study of history, the fact that this book is a graphic history is very appealing—it sets the tone for the course at the beginning, and it allows me to push the students to read more 'difficult' texts."

JAMES DE LORENZI, *City University of New York, John Jay College*

"There is no book like this that combines primary and secondary material in a way that encourages students to engage with the process of 'making history.' It forces the students to confront the process of turning historical documents into narrative history in ways that few other texts do. It provides the background information necessary to understand the case study from rural Ghana, while also asking students whether they think the author has appropriately interpreted the source. It is a gem of a pedagogical text that is also historically useful and relevant to understanding slavery and social systems in the late 19th century."

JOHN AERNI-FLESSNER, *Michigan State University*

"Students like *Abina* because it defies their ideas of what a 'real' history book should be, but they end up thinking critically and historically about the content in ways that do not always occur with other books."

ERIK GILBERT, *Arkansas State University*

"One of the key advantages of this book is that the graphic text does not stand on its own; the author gives the reader a chance to engage the courts transcript as well, to grapple with his own interpretation of the text, and to consider how the silences in historical record impact the reconstructions of Abina's life story. This is an effective text for highlighting the limits of historical knowledge and to remove that gatekeeper/expertise stance that is commonplace in the historical profession. The reader becomes a part of the text in an important way and can contribute to the interpretation of the text."

FIONA VERNAL, *University of Connecticut*

"I allow students to craft their own four-page writing assignment using the graphic novel and one of the supplementary sections, and the variety of work students turn out is impressive."

JASON McCOLLOM, *University of Arkansas*

"I think *Abina* is really wonderful for helping students understand the legal processes that were central to the construction of modern empires, in a narrative that is far more compelling than any text I have encountered."

MICHAEL McINNESHIN, *La Salle University*

"*Abina and the Important Men* is a thoughtful exercise that explicitly takes the reader 'behind-the-scenes' to understand how historical narratives are forged and constructed."

PETER A. DYKEMA, *Arkansas Tech University*

ABINA | AND THE IMPORTANT MEN

A GRAPHIC HISTORY

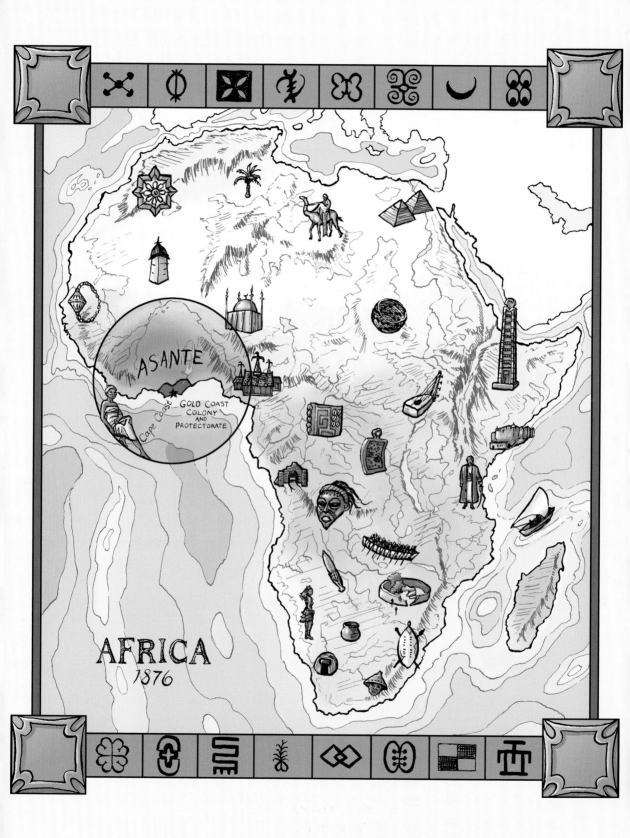

ASANTE

Cape Coast

GOLD COAST
COLONY
AND
PROTECTORATE

AFRICA
1876

ABINA | AND THE IMPORTANT MEN

A GRAPHIC HISTORY

SECOND EDITION

TREVOR R. GETZ

LIZ CLARKE

New York   Oxford

Oxford University Press

Oxford University Press is a department of the University of Oxford.
It furthers the University's objective of excellence in research,
scholarship, and education by publishing worldwide.

Oxford   New York
Auckland   Cape Town   Dar es Salaam   Hong Kong   Karachi
Kuala Lumpur   Madrid   Melbourne   Mexico City   Nairobi
New Delhi   Shanghai   Taipei   Toronto

With offices in
Argentina   Austria   Brazil   Chile   Czech Republic   France   Greece
Guatemala   Hungary   Italy   Japan   Poland   Portugal   Singapore
South Korea   Switzerland   Thailand   Turkey   Ukraine   Vietnam

For titles covered by Section 112 of the US Higher Education
Opportunity Act, please visit www.oup.com/us/he for the latest
information about pricing and alternate formats.

Published by Oxford University Press
198 Madison Avenue, New York, New York 10016
http://www.oup.com

Oxford is a registered trademark of Oxford University Press.

Library of Congress Cataloging-in-Publication Data
Getz, Trevor R., author.
  Abina and the important men : a graphic history / Trevor R. Getz, Liz Clarke.—Second edition.
    pages cm
  ISBN 978-0-19-023874-2 (pbk., acid-free : alk. paper)   1.   Mansah, Abina—Trials, litigation, etc.—
Comic books, strips, etc.   2.   Slavery—Law and legislation—Ghana—History—19th century—
Comic books, strips, etc.   3.   Women slaves—Ghana—History—19th century—Comic books,
strips, etc.   I. Clarke, Liz (Illustrator) II. Title.
  KRX46.M36G48 2015
  306.3'62092—dc23
                        2014042375

Printing number: 9 8 7 6

Printed in the United States of America
on acid-free paper

For Kaela Getz, who—like Abina Mansah—won't be pushed around

CONTENTS

MAPS AND FIGURES

LETTER TO THE READER

Dear Reader,

    This graphic history recounts the life story of Abina Mansah, a young woman who lived in West Africa during the late nineteenth century. She is representative of the largest group of our human ancestors: those who left little but physical evidence behind to help us to remember them. The histories of all societies, whether passed down orally or in written documents, usually focus on just the major political and social figures. Ordinary peasants and townspeople rarely appear in the record. Even social histories composed by professional historians in the past few decades have tended to focus on everyday people only as a group, instead of as individuals. There are many reasons for this limited perspective on the past. For most of history, men and women of the middle and lower classes were illiterate or wrote little. Even when they left behind written records, these were perceived as having little value and were not carefully preserved. Because of this, their voices faded into oblivion. But historians have also been responsible for this silence: They have tended to see ordinary individuals as less important, and so they have often chosen not to write about them.

    In the last few decades, however, historians have developed new strategies for learning about the experiences and perspectives of "**people without history.**" They have learned to use new sources, oral traditions, archaeological remains, and the records of how words and languages have changed over time to gain insight into the lives of the silent and the forgotten. They have also developed novel ways of finding common peoples' voices in the margins of older sources, such as court cases and newspapers. Many scholarly books and articles have been written about the lives of everyday individuals as a result of these new sources and techniques. Yet, ironically, most of them are not accessible to general audiences today because they are presented in scholarly jargon, published in specialized journals, and designed to be read only by other historians and academics. These works generally seek to be *critical*—that is, to raise complex but sometimes esoteric questions about lived experiences. Those life histories that *are* accessible to the general public tend to be overly simplistic, to cater to nationalist or group-identity goals, or, worse, are simply incorrect. These narratives seek to be *celebratory*—that is, to commemorate a lived experience in order to promote a particular worldview or identity.

Abina and the Important Men is one of a number of projects that seeks to find a middle ground between scholarly and popular histories of regular people. It is not a work of *historical fiction*, but instead a *history* because it aims for accuracy and authenticity even while recognizing that all historical works are at some level speculative and subjective. It is neither completely celebratory nor wholly critical; instead it attempts to show how these two impulses can be linked together. In order to achieve this careful balancing act, it consists of four different approaches to the story. First, at its heart, *Abina* is a graphic history that through pictures and texts presents an interpretation of the life of an African woman, Abina Mansah, based on the single source in which she appeared: the transcript of an 1876 court case. Second, following the graphic history, it contains the transcript itself, included so that the reader can hear as close as possible Abina's own voice and can evaluate the author's and illustrator's interpretations of her story (presented in original form starting on page 85). Third, this volume includes a historical reconstruction of the world in which Abina lived so that the reader can place the transcript and the graphic history within the context of the time and place in which they are set (beginning on page 113). Fourth, rather than seeking to be the final authority on this story, it invites the reader to question the authors' interpretations in a section that raises key issues about the ways in which historians work to interpret the past (beginning on page 133).

This is the second edition of *Abina and the Important Men*. It includes a new section, Part 5 ("Engaging Abina"), built on the contributions and ideas of numerous students, readers, and scholars who have used the first edition. This new edition features a number of small changes and two innovative sections, a look at the way that greater attention to gender shifts our understanding of Abina's experiences, and a debate between three leading historians about whether Abina was a slave. It also contains additional testimony, previously lost but now rediscovered in the National Archives of Ghana.

We see this work as a conversation we are having with Abina Mansah. We invite you to join in as well.

Trevor Getz
Historian and Author

Liz Clarke
Graphic Artist and Illustrator

ACKNOWLEDGMENTS

The author would like to acknowledge the assistance and support of everyone who read, reviewed, and supported the development of this project, including these reviewers of the manuscript: Timothy Carmichael, College of Charleston; Alicia Decker, Purdue University; Nicola Foote, Florida Gulf Coast University; Tiffany Jones, California State University–San Bernardino; Paul Landau, University of Maryland; Maxim Matusevich, Seton Hall University; Erin O'Connor, Bridgewater State University; Jennifer Popiel, St. Louis University; Jonathan Reynolds, Northern Kentucky University; Jeremy Rich, Middle Tennessee State University; Jason Ripper, Everett Community College; Sharlene Sayegh, California State University, Long Beach.

Special thanks are due to Provost Sue Rosser and the Office of Research and Sponsored Programs at San Francisco State University for funding the initial development of this project. Patrick Manning, Jonathan Reynolds, Paul Lovejoy, Candace Goucher, Heather Streets-Salter, Martin Klein, Kwasi Konadu, Abena Osseo-Asare, and Ken O'Donnell reviewed the entire manuscript. Students in the history departments of Northern Kentucky University and San Francisco State tested and commented on the manuscript. At Oxford, project editor Marianne Paul managed the production of the manuscript with grace and agility, and Dan Niver, designer, created a visual setting that captures Abina's spirit and humanity.

The second edition of this volume owes its existence to expert reviews, responses, and contributions by scholars like Emmanuel Akyeampong, Maryanne Rhett, Jonathan Reynolds, Manu Herbstein, Sarah Hepburn, Erik Gilbert, Natalia R.L. Bassi, Michael A. Chaney, and Akosua Darkwah. Several high school teachers and their classes played a big role as well, especially Liz Leidel, Christy Story, and David Sherrin. We owe an even more enormous debt to our contributors: Kwasi Konadu, Sandra Greene, and Antoinette Burton.

This second edition also would not have been possible without the support of Charles Cavaliere, editor extraordinaire at Oxford University Press. Charles immediately recognized the project's potential and worked tirelessly to see the first edition come to life. He has played a key role in creating this deeper, richer version as well.

REVIEWERS OF THE SECOND EDITION

John Aerni-Flessner, Michigan State University
William E. Burns, George Washington University
Kenneth R. Curtis, CSU Long Beach
James De Lorenzi, CUNY John Jay College
Alicia C. Decker, Penn State University
Peter A. Dykema, Arkansas Tech University
Erik Gilbert, Arkansas State University
Aaron Gulyas, Mott Community College
Jason McCollom, University of Arkansas
Chris Padgett, American River College
Charles V. Reed, Elizabeth City State University
Maryanne Rhett, Monmouth University
Jason Ripper, Everett Community College
Fiona Vernal, University of Connecticut
Sarah Zimmerman, Western Washington University

A NOTE ON GHANAIAN IDEOGRAMS, SPELLING CONVENTIONS, AND NAMES

The symbols that begin each part of this book are Ghanaian *adinkra* ideograms. They are each accompanied by the Twi (Akan) language proverb or saying that they represent and an English translation. Adinkra are usually employed as metaphors, and that is the role they play here. The reader is invited to ponder the complexities of their meanings in relation to the text that follows.

Some combinations of letters are pronounced differently in the Twi language. "Dw" sounds like a short, hard "j" sound, and "ky" produces a "ch" sound. Also, Twi has a slightly expanded alphabet with two extra letters: The letter "ɔ" is pronounced much like the "o" in *pot*, and "ɛ" is pronounced much like the "e" in *set*. In writing Twi words in English, these letters are often replaced by "o" and "e," respectively, and we follow that convention in this volume. However, we will note here that *chief* can be written *ohene* or *ɔhene* and domestic slave might be written *odonko* or *odonkɔ*.

Finally, we have chosen to represent the names of Abina and other actors in this story as they are spelled in the court transcript, in order to avoid confusion. However, these are not the common modern spellings of these names. Therefore, we list the names of individuals in this story alongside their modern analogs here.

Abina Mansah: Abena Mensah/Mansa
Quamina Eddoo: Kwamena Adu/Edu
Eccoah Coom: Akua Kuma
Adjuah N'Yamiwhah: Adwoa Nyamewa
Yowahwah/Yawahwah: Yaw Awua/Awoah
Edoo Buffoe: Adu Bɔfoɔ/Bofo/Bafo

PART I
THE GRAPHIC
HISTORY

FAWOHODIE
"INDEPENDENCE"

CHAPTER 1

ABINA AWAKES

THE GOLD COAST OF WEST AFRICA, 1876.

ONCE RULED BY THE MIGHTY ASANTE CONFEDERATION, WHOSE KINGS HELD SWAY FROM THE SEA ACROSS THE GREAT FORESTS AND DEEP INTO THE SAVANNA OF THE WEST AFRICAN INTERIOR.

BUT THE ASANTE KINGS WERE DEFEATED BY THE BRITISH AND THEIR ALLIES--THE CITIZENS OF SEVERAL SMALL TOWNS AND CHIEFDOMS-- IN A GREAT WAR BETWEEN 1873 AND 1874, AND PUSHED BACK FROM THE COAST.

ASANTE CONFEDERATION

• Kumasi

THE PROTECTORATE

THE COLONY

ADANSI

Volta

ACCRA

Tano

Saltpond

Cape Coast

Elmina

NOW, GOLD COAST IS RULED BY THE BRITISH, WHO HAVE DIVIDED IT INTO THE SMALL COASTAL STRIP KNOWN AS THE COLONY AND THE TECHNICALLY INDEPENDENT BUT SUBORDINATE CHIEFDOMS OF THE PROTECTORATE.

THE BIGGEST PRIZE WON BY BRITAIN IS CONTROL OVER LOCAL TRADE. ONCE, THIS HAD MEANT GOLD AND ENSLAVED HUMANS...

NOW, HOWEVER, THE GOLD TRADE HAS DRIED UP, WHILE BRITAIN HAS TURNED FROM THE WORLD'S LARGEST SLAVE-TRADING STATE INTO AN ABOLITIONIST POWER...THE NEW GOLD IS PALM OIL, HARVESTED IN THE GOLD COAST AND VITAL TO THE FUNCTIONING OF BRITAIN'S GROWING INDUSTRIAL PRODUCTION.

5

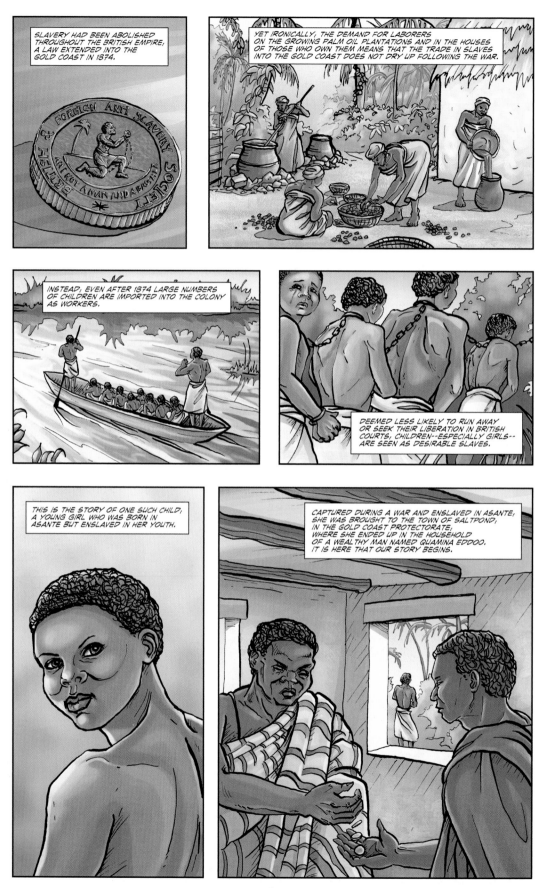

SLAVERY HAD BEEN ABOLISHED THROUGHOUT THE BRITISH EMPIRE, A LAW EXTENDED INTO THE GOLD COAST IN 1874.

YET IRONICALLY, THE DEMAND FOR LABORERS ON THE GROWING PALM OIL PLANTATIONS AND IN THE HOUSES OF THOSE WHO OWN THEM MEANS THAT THE TRADE IN SLAVES INTO THE GOLD COAST DOES NOT DRY UP FOLLOWING THE WAR.

INSTEAD, EVEN AFTER 1874 LARGE NUMBERS OF CHILDREN ARE IMPORTED INTO THE COLONY AS WORKERS.

DEEMED LESS LIKELY TO RUN AWAY OR SEEK THEIR LIBERATION IN BRITISH COURTS, CHILDREN--ESPECIALLY GIRLS-- ARE SEEN AS DESIRABLE SLAVES.

THIS IS THE STORY OF ONE SUCH CHILD; A YOUNG GIRL WHO WAS BORN IN ASANTE BUT ENSLAVED IN HER YOUTH.

CAPTURED DURING A WAR AND ENSLAVED IN ASANTE, SHE WAS BROUGHT TO THE TOWN OF SALTPOND, IN THE GOLD COAST PROTECTORATE, WHERE SHE ENDED UP IN THE HOUSEHOLD OF A WEALTHY MAN NAMED QUAMINA EDDOO. IT IS HERE THAT OUR STORY BEGINS.

8

THEN LISTEN QUICKLY. IF THE POLICE FIND YOU WANDERING AROUND THEY CAN PUT YOU IN PRISON. AND THERE ARE WORSE THINGS-- MEN WHO WOULD TAKE A GIRL LIKE YOU AND RUIN YOU.

I THOUGHT EVERYONE HERE WAS FREE.

WHAT IS FREE? YOU CAN GET A PIECE OF PAPER SAYING YOU'RE FREE, AND THEN YOU CAN LEAVE ANYTIME YOU WANT.

BUT THE BRITISH DON'T WANT YOU HERE IF YOU DON'T HAVE A JOB AND A PLACE TO STAY. YOU MUST FIND A PLACE TO BELONG.

THEN I WILL FIND ONE. CAN YOU HELP ME?

I KNOW SOMEONE WHO WORKS FOR THE BRITISH. HE, TOO, IS AN IMPORTANT MAN.

MAYBE HE CAN HELP YOU WITH A JOB, AND HELP YOU GET YOUR PAPERS AS WELL.

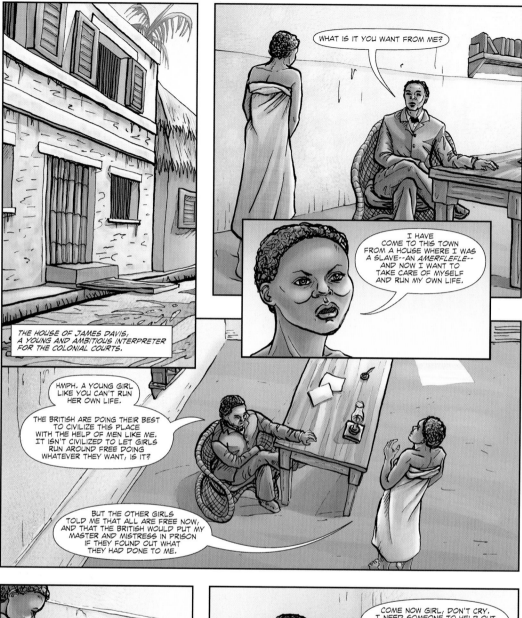

WHAT IS IT YOU WANT FROM ME?

I HAVE COME TO THIS TOWN FROM A HOUSE WHERE I WAS A SLAVE--AN *AMERFLEFLE*--AND NOW I WANT TO TAKE CARE OF MYSELF AND RUN MY OWN LIFE.

THE HOUSE OF JAMES DAVIS, A YOUNG AND AMBITIOUS INTERPRETER FOR THE COLONIAL COURTS.

HMPH. A YOUNG GIRL LIKE YOU CAN'T RUN HER OWN LIFE.

THE BRITISH ARE DOING THEIR BEST TO CIVILIZE THIS PLACE WITH THE HELP OF MEN LIKE ME. IT ISN'T CIVILIZED TO LET GIRLS RUN AROUND FREE DOING WHATEVER THEY WANT, IS IT?

BUT THE OTHER GIRLS TOLD ME THAT ALL ARE FREE NOW, AND THAT THE BRITISH WOULD PUT MY MASTER AND MISTRESS IN PRISON IF THEY FOUND OUT WHAT THEY HAD DONE TO ME.

WELL, IT'S TRUE THAT THERE IS NO LEGAL SLAVERY HERE IN CAPE COAST, OR THROUGHOUT THE COLONY AND PROTECTORATE.

BUT LOOK, THE GOVERNMENT DOESN'T HAVE THE MONEY OR THE ABILITY TO ENFORCE THE LAW EVERYWHERE.

COME NOW GIRL, DON'T CRY. I NEED SOMEONE TO HELP OUT AROUND HERE. YOU CAN BE MY MAID, AND MAKE A LITTLE MONEY, AND STAY HERE.

SO LONG AS YOU NEVER LEAVE CAPE COAST, YOU SHOULD BE SAFE FROM YOUR MASTER.

11

12

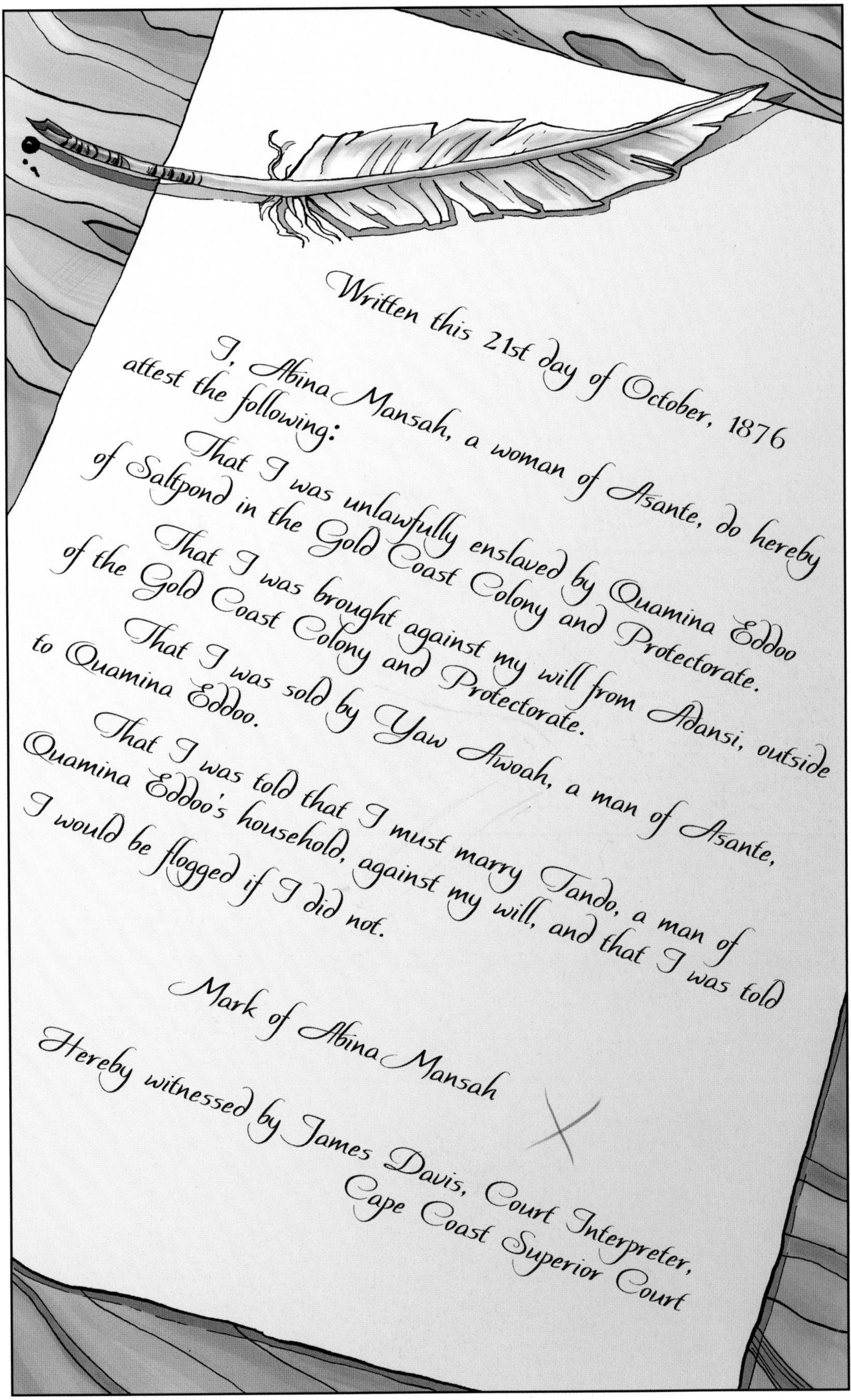

Written this 21st day of October, 1876

I, Abina Mansah, a woman of Asante, do hereby attest the following:

That I was unlawfully enslaved by Quamina Eddoo of Saltpond in the Gold Coast Colony and Protectorate.

That I was brought against my will from Adansi, outside of the Gold Coast Colony and Protectorate.

That I was sold by Yaw Awoah, a man of Asante, to Quamina Eddoo.

That I was told that I must marry Tando, a man of Quamina Eddoo's household, against my will, and that I was told I would be flogged if I did not.

Mark of Abina Mansah

X

Hereby witnessed by James Davis, Court Interpreter, Cape Coast Superior Court

13

THE NEXT MORNING, IN THE CHAMBERS OF ACTING JUDICIAL ASSESSOR WILLIAM MELTON.

YOU'VE NEVER TAKEN AN INTEREST IN THESE CASES BEFORE, DAVIS.

WHAT'S SO SPECIAL ABOUT THIS ONE?

SHE CAME TO ME, SIR, AND CONVINCED ME THAT THIS WAS RIGHT.

SHE'S ONLY A GIRL, AND SHE'S SCARED OUT OF HER WITS.

BUT YOU PUT ME IN A BAD POSITION.
ON THE ONE HAND, HER MAJESTY HAS OUTLAWED SLAVERY--AND ESPECIALLY THE IMPORTATION OF SLAVES FROM ASANTE.

ON THE OTHER HAND, WE DON'T WANT TO STIR THINGS UP. WE CAN'T AFFORD TO HAVE SLAVE OWNERS BECOMING ANGRY WITH US... NOT WHEN THINGS ARE SO STIRRED UP STILL FROM THE LAST WAR.

MOREOVER, MEN LIKE QUAMINA EDDOO GROW PALM OIL, AND PALM OIL IS TAXED, AND THOSE TAXES PAY YOUR SALARY AND, IN THE LONG RUN, MINE AS WELL.

THIS IS SIMPLY TOO BIG.

SIR, WHEN I WAS A CHILD I KNEW NOTHING OF BRITAIN OR OF CHRISTIANITY.

BUT MY FATHER SENT ME TO SCHOOL TO BECOME A CHRISTIAN, AND THEN I CAME TO KNOW EVERYTHING BRITAIN STANDS FOR... INCLUDING THE ABOLITION OF SLAVERY.

SURELY, IF THE BRITISH STAND FOR RIGHTEOUSNESS, WE SHOULD AT LEAST GIVE THE GIRL HER TRIAL?

UM...VERY WELL. I'LL SEND A CONSTABLE TO FIND THIS QUAMINA EDDOO. HIS PLANTATION ISN'T FAR AWAY.

IF NOTHING ELSE, THIS CHILD CAN HAVE HER DAY IN COURT.

I'LL SEND CONSTABLE MOOSA TO BRING HIM IN. THAT'S HIS DISTRICT.

CHAPTER 2
THE BREAKING OF THE BEADS

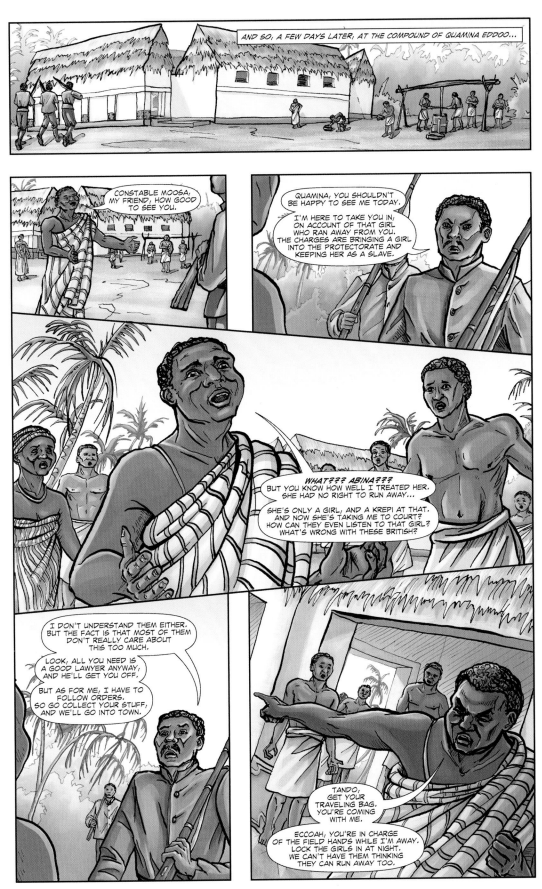

DON'T WORRY, MY BROTHER. YOU CAN COUNT ON ME.

I'LL MAKE SURE THEY DON'T FOLLOW IN THE FOOTSTEPS OF THAT LITTLE SLAVE!

THE HOME OF JAMES HUTTON BREW, DESCENDANT OF SCOTTISH TRADERS AND AFRICAN CHIEFS.
AN EDUCATED MAN, A CHRISTIAN, AND A SOMETIME EMPLOYEE OF THE COLONIAL GOVERNMENT.

HE IS ONE OF THE FEW TRAINED LAWYERS IN ACCRA.

I TELL YOU JAMES, IF I KNEW THEY WERE GOING TO OUTLAW SLAVERY I WOULD NEVER HAVE SUPPORTED THE BRITISH IN THE WAR AGAINST ASANTE.

AT THE TIME, THEY PROMISED JUST TO BE OUR ALLIES. BUT SINCE THEN, THEY HAVE SOMEHOW FORCED US TO AGREE TO THEIR LAWS AND TO PAY TAXES TO THEM.

WELL, YOU HAVE TO BLAME THE AHENFO--THE CHIEFS. ONE MOMENT THEY WERE SAYING THEY WERE JUST GOING TO FIGHT ALONGSIDE THE BRITISH AS ALLIES, AND THE NEXT THEY AGREE TO FOLLOW ALL OF THESE LAWS.

I GUESS IT'S BECAUSE THEY'RE STILL AFRAID OF ASANTE, BUT I ALSO HEAR SOME OF THEM ARE ACCEPTING SALARIES AND GIFTS FROM THE BRITISH.

BUT FOR WHATEVER REASON, THE FACT IS THAT YOUR CHIEF, LIKE THE OTHERS, AGREED THAT SLAVERY IS OUTLAWED AND THAT THE BRITISH COURTS CAN TRY ANYONE WHO KEEPS A SLAVE.

"I DON'T REMEMBER MUCH OF MY CHILDHOOD. I WAS BORN IN KREPI, IN EWELAND."

"WHAT I CAN REMEMBER OF MY YOUNG CHILDHOOD IS COOKING WITH MY MOTHER, MAKING FUFU. I HAD MANY BROTHERS AND SISTERS."

"THEN THERE WAS A WAR, AND I REMEMBER THAT A GENERAL NAMED ADU BOFO CAPTURED ME. I LIVED WITH HIM UNTIL HE SOLD ME TO ANOTHER MAN IN ADANSI PROVINCE."

AS A SLAVE?

I SUPPOSE YOU WOULD SAY THAT... BUT WE SAID *ODONKO* IN THE ASANTE LANGUAGE, OR *AMERFLEFLE* IN EWE, WHICH MEANS SOMEONE WHO IS BOUGHT.

"THEN THERE WAS ANOTHER WAR, AND I WAS STOLEN AGAIN, AND SOLD TO A MAN NAMED YAW AWOAH. HE TOLD ME I WAS MARRIED TO HIM, AND THAT AS HIS WIFE I WOULD HELP HIM TO CARRY GOODS FOR SALE IN THE BRITISH COLONY."

22

PUT ON THESE CLOTHS I HAVE BROUGHT FOR YOU, GIRL, SO THAT YOU MAY GO TO YOUR NEW HUSBAND TANDO A CLOTHED WOMAN.

HOW CAN YOU GIVE ME TO TANDO? I DO NOT BELONG TO YOU! I AM A MARRIED WOMAN ALREADY.

"BUT ABOUT TEN DAYS AFTER, QUAMINA EDDOO GAVE ME TWO CLOTHS AND TOLD ME THAT HE HAD GIVEN ME IN MARRIAGE TO ONE OF HIS HOUSE PEOPLE."

SILLY GIRL, YOU ARE NO LONGER MARRIED TO YAW AWOA.

HE HAS SOLD YOU TO ME AND I CAN DO WITH YOU WHAT I WANT.

THEN MY HEART WAS TORN.

I HAD BEEN BORN TO A FAMILY, AND THEN ENSLAVED IN A WAR -- TWICE. WHEN THINGS WERE DARKEST, YAW AWOAH HAD BOUGHT ME, AND MADE ME HIS WIFE, AND THINGS WERE BETTER. BUT NOW I KNEW FOR SURE HE HAD LIED TO ME, AND SOLD ME.

I WAS A SLAVE ONCE MORE.

24

CHAPTER 3
THE TRUTH

WHAT IS THIS ABOUT CLOTHS AND BEADS? CAN YOU EXPLAIN?

THE PEOPLE OF THE BUSH HAVE A CUSTOM THAT THE GIVING OF CLOTH SIGNIFIES BELONGING--A FATHER GIVES CLOTH TO A CHILD, FOR EXAMPLE, OR A HUSBAND TO A WIFE. OR EVEN A MASTER TO A SERVANT.

THIS IS WHY THE WOMEN WHO OWN STALLS IN THE MARKETPLACE BUY THEIR OWN CLOTH, AND LOTS OF IT... TO SHOW THEY ARE INDEPENDENT.

WHEN YAW AWOAH CUT THE WITNESS'S OLD BEADS AWAY, AND THEN QUAMINA EDDOO GAVE HER NEW CLOTH, THEY WERE TELLING HER THAT SHE BELONGED TO EDDOO NOW.

MAYBE ALSO SOME OF THE CLOTH WAS FROM TANDO, AS HE WAS TO BE HER HUSBAND, AND SO SHE WAS TO BELONG TO HIM AS WELL...

YES, BUT AS YOU SAY, THE GIVING OF CLOTH DOESN'T NECESSARILY INDICATE SLAVERY.

IN FACT, AS MY CLIENT WILL TESTIFY, GIFTS OF CLOTH ARE OFTEN GIVEN TO GUESTS.

IF THIS HAD BEEN A CASE OF SLAVERY, OTHER CEREMONIES WOULD HAVE BEEN OBSERVED.

ABINA, YOU HAVE SEEN HOW SLAVES ARE SOLD, RIGHT? ARE THERE USUALLY CEREMONIES WHEN THEY ARE HANDED OVER?

YES.

WERE ANY OF THESE OBSERVED WHEN YOU WERE ALLEGEDLY SOLD TO EDDOO?

THE ONLY THING THAT WAS DONE WAS THE CUTTING OF THE BEADS.

29

34

ISN'T IT TRUE THAT THEY ARE NOT HERE TODAY BECAUSE THEY ARE ALL FREE, JUST AS WERE YOU WHEN YOU LIVED IN THAT HOUSE?

YOU KNEW YOU WERE FREE, DIDN'T YOU!

I DID NOT KNOW IT.

ARE YOU AWARE THAT EVERYBODY IN THE PROTECTORATE IS FREED AND THAT THOSE PEOPLE YOU SAW IN THE DEFENDANT'S HOUSE ARE AS FREE AS THE DEFENDANT, OR MR. DAVIS, OR I ?

MANY OF THE PEOPLE LIVING IN THAT HOUSE ARE THE CHILDREN OF THE SLAVES.

MAYBE, BUT THEY WERE NOT SLAVES THEMSELVES, WERE THEY?

THEY WERE NOT ALL FREE. SOME WERE SLAVES.

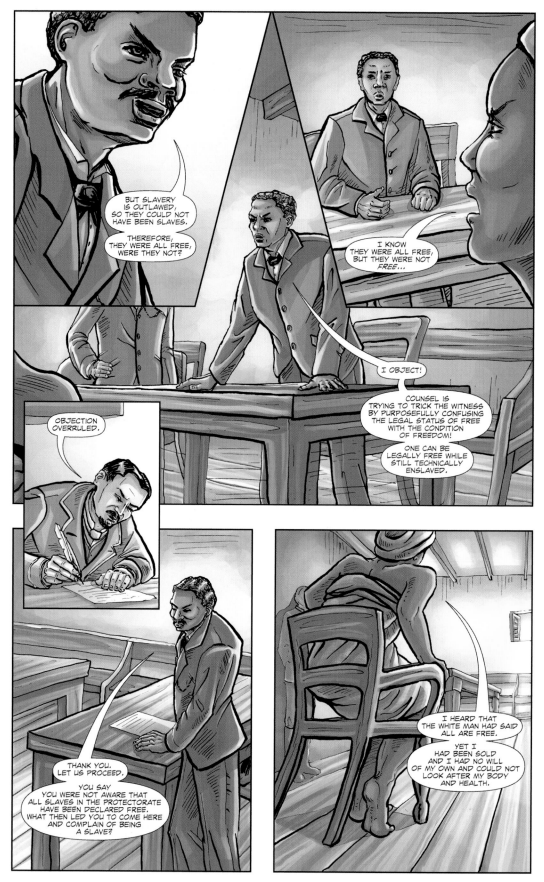

CHAPTER 4
LIFE AT QUAMINA EDDOO'S HOUSE

41

43

44

45

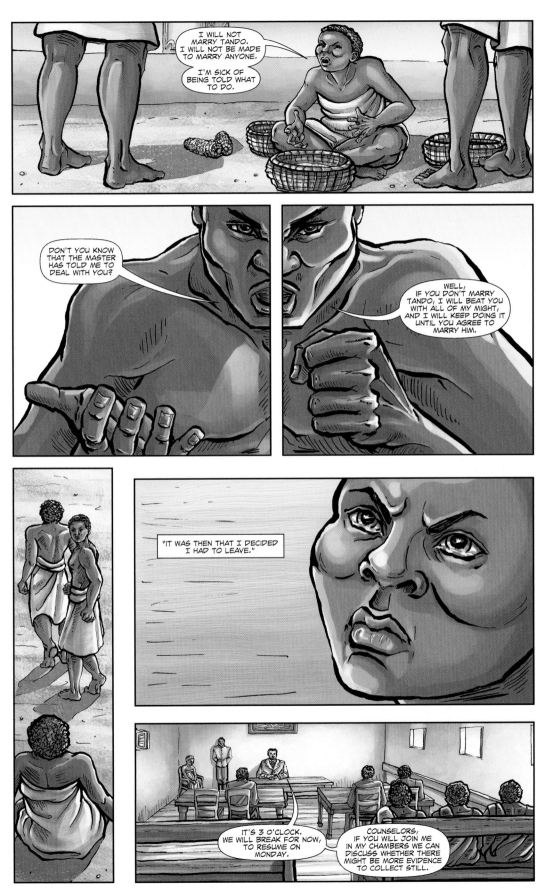

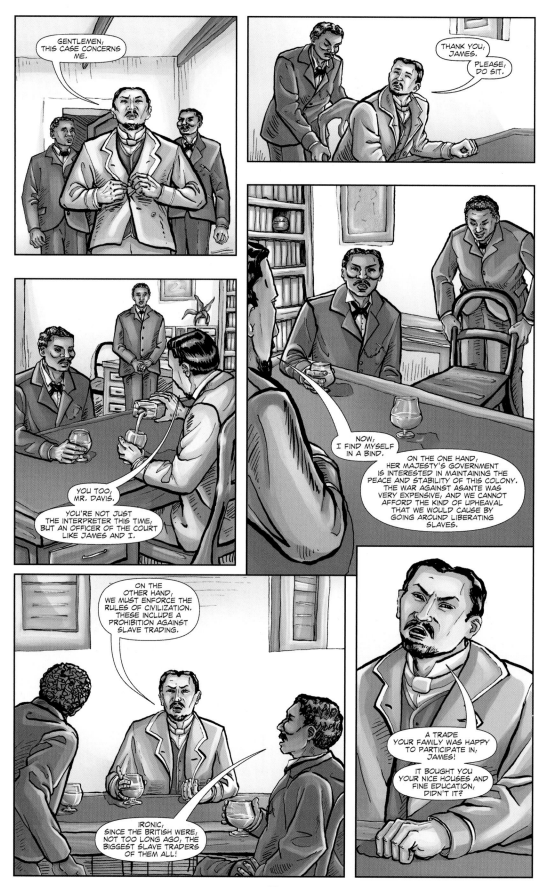

49

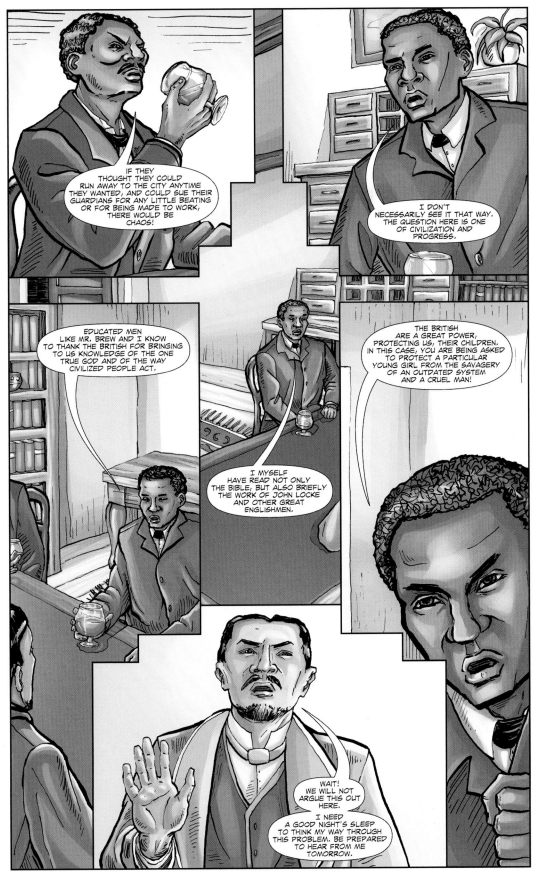

HE DID NOTHING GOOD FOR ME

55

BUT THERE'S A SECOND PART TO THIS DOCUMENT.

"IN ORDER TO GATHER MORE EVIDENCE, I AM REQUESTING THAT THE FOLLOWING PEOPLE APPEAR IN COURT VOLUNTARILY..."

...two men of the household of Quamina Eddoo, namely Atta and Senegay...

...and the girls Accosuah, Adjua, Abina, and Amba.

THIS IS GOOD FOR US, ISN'T IT?

IT'S MIXED. I DON'T THINK THIS JURY WILL BE SYMPATHETIC. TOO MANY OF THEM ARE SLAVE OWNERS OR HAVE FRIENDS WHO ARE.

BUT PERHAPS THE TESTIMONY OF THESE WITNESSES CAN HELP US OUT.

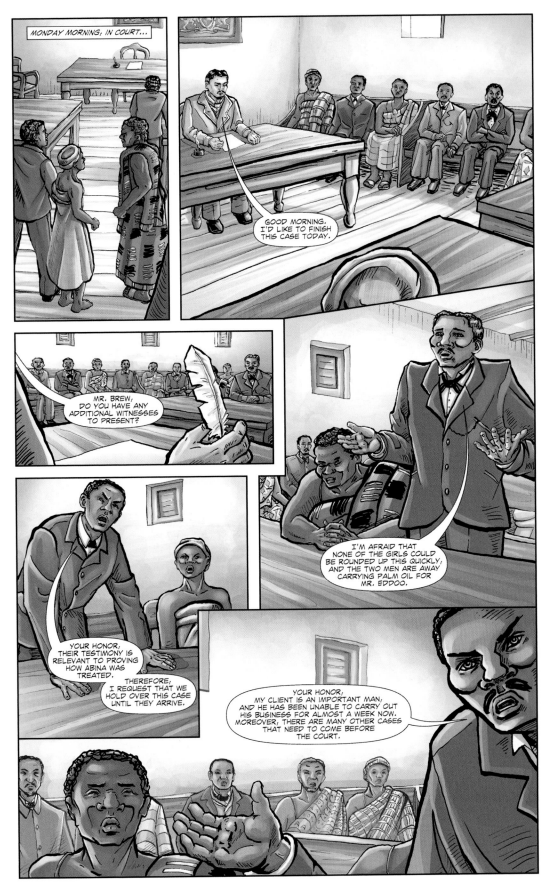

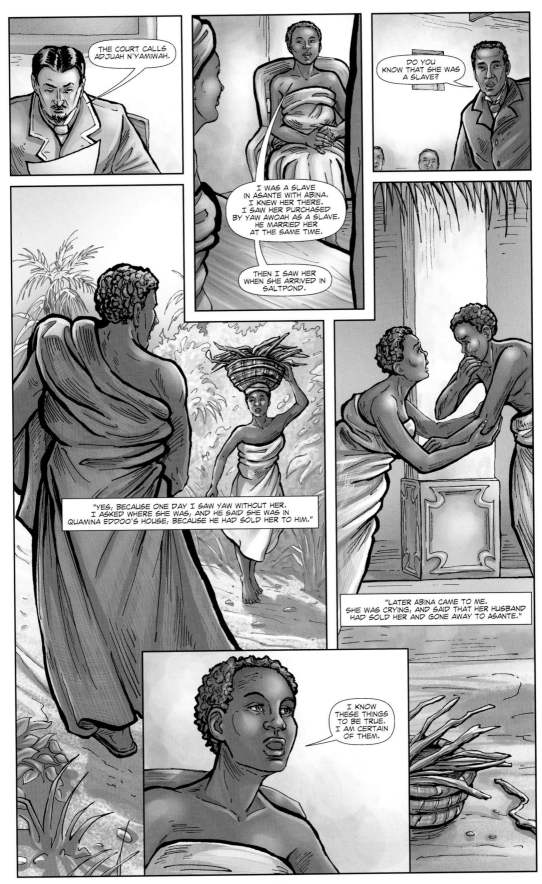

WELL, WE HAVE EXHAUSTED OUR WITNESS LIST.

AT THIS TIME, COURT IS ADJOURNED SO THAT I MAY CONFER WITH THE JURY.

WE WILL ANNOUNCE OUR VERDICT TOMORROW.

DO YOU THINK WE HAVE A CHANCE?

I DON'T KNOW.

IT WAS A PRETTY MEAN TRICK TO PULL, KEEPING THE OTHER WITNESSES AWAY...

...AND THE JURY DOESN'T SEEM SYMPATHETIC TO US.

BUT I *MUST* BELIEVE WE CAN RELY ON ENGLISH JUSTICE!

CHAPTER 6
ABINA SILENCED, ABINA REDEEMED

ALL DAY, ALL OVER THE GOLD COAST COLONY AND PROTECTORATE, PEOPLE GO ABOUT THEIR BUSINESS.

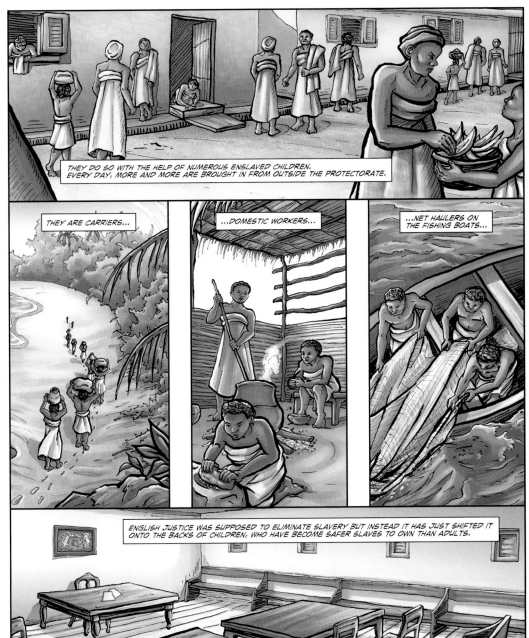

THEY DO SO WITH THE HELP OF NUMEROUS ENSLAVED CHILDREN. EVERY DAY, MORE AND MORE ARE BROUGHT IN FROM OUTSIDE THE PROTECTORATE.

THEY ARE CARRIERS...

...DOMESTIC WORKERS...

...NET HAULERS ON THE FISHING BOATS...

ENGLISH JUSTICE WAS SUPPOSED TO ELIMINATE SLAVERY BUT INSTEAD IT HAS JUST SHIFTED IT ONTO THE BACKS OF CHILDREN, WHO HAVE BECOME SAFER SLAVES TO OWN THAN ADULTS.

THE CASE BEFORE MAGISTRATE MELTON COULD IMPACT ALL OF THEM...

...BUT FOR ONE YOUNG WOMAN, IT'S PERSONAL.

IT'S ABOUT HER OWN STORY, AND HER OWN SUFFERING, AND HER OWN JUSTICE...

...AND WHO IS THIS GROUP OF IMPORTANT MEN?

WHAT DO THEY KNOW OF SUFFERING? OF FREEDOM?

THOMAS AMINISSAH. A LANDOWNER AND LEADING MEMBER OF THE WESLEYAN METHODIST CONGREGATION.

JONATHAN DAWSON, A TRADER IN PALM OIL. SON OF A BRITISH MERCHANT AND GRANDSON OF A CHIEF.

IN THE ABSENCE OF EVIDENCE THAT SHE WAS MISTREATED, IT SEEMS TO ME THAT QUAMINA EDDOO ACTED MUCH LIKE A FATHER TO THAT GIRL.

DID HE NOT FEED HER AND CLOTHE HER? CERTAINLY HE DISCIPLINED HER, BUT WAS SHE NOT DISOBEDIENT?

I'M NOT SURE THAT HE WAS A WONDERFUL FATHER--A BIT ROUGH WITH HER, PERHAPS.

BUT HAVE YOU CONSIDERED THE CHILLING EFFECT OF PUNISHING A MAN LIKE QUAMINA EDDOO?

IT IS OUR DUTY, OF COURSE, TO FREE THE SLAVES. OUR BELOVED LEADER, JOHN WESLEY, TELLS US THAT.

HOWEVER, DUMPING THESE YOUNG GIRLS ONTO THE STREETS TO BECOME VAGRANTS DOES NO FAVORS TO THEM OR TO ANYONE ELSE...

72

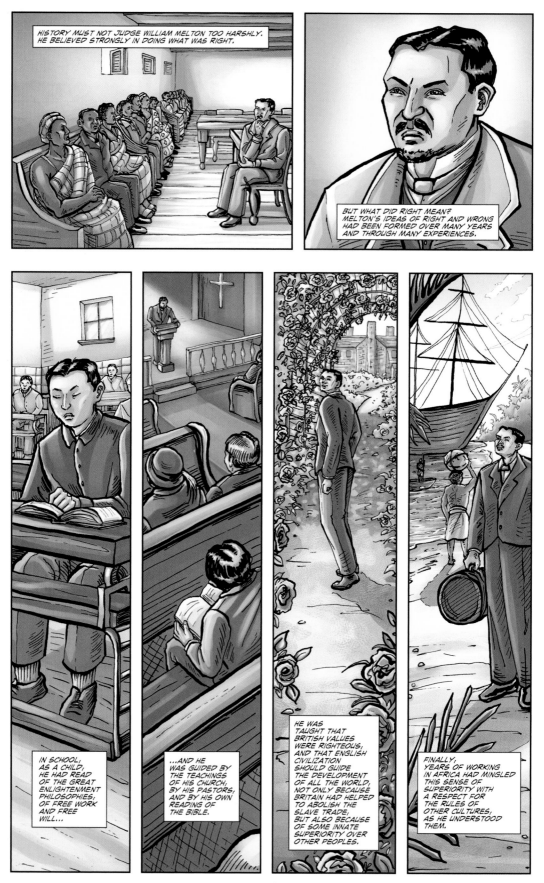

HISTORY MUST NOT JUDGE WILLIAM MELTON TOO HARSHLY. HE BELIEVED STRONGLY IN DOING WHAT WAS RIGHT.

BUT WHAT DID RIGHT MEAN? MELTON'S IDEAS OF RIGHT AND WRONG HAD BEEN FORMED OVER MANY YEARS AND THROUGH MANY EXPERIENCES.

IN SCHOOL, AS A CHILD, HE HAD READ OF THE GREAT ENLIGHTENMENT PHILOSOPHIES, OF FREE WORK AND FREE WILL...

...AND HE WAS GUIDED BY THE TEACHINGS OF HIS CHURCH, BY HIS PASTORS, AND BY HIS OWN READING OF THE BIBLE.

HE WAS TAUGHT THAT BRITISH VALUES WERE RIGHTEOUS, AND THAT ENGLISH CIVILIZATION SHOULD GUIDE THE DEVELOPMENT OF ALL THE WORLD, NOT ONLY BECAUSE BRITAIN HAD HELPED TO ABOLISH THE SLAVE TRADE, BUT ALSO BECAUSE OF SOME INNATE SUPERIORITY OVER OTHER PEOPLES.

FINALLY, YEARS OF WORKING IN AFRICA HAD MINGLED THIS SENSE OF SUPERIORITY WITH A RESPECT FOR THE RULES OF OTHER CULTURES, AS HE UNDERSTOOD THEM.

YET MELTON HAD TWO GREAT WEAKNESSES THAT ALLOWED HIM TO BE EASILY MANIPULATED BY POWERFUL LOCAL MEN.

FIRST, HE BELIEVED THAT HE UNDERSTOOD LOCAL CULTURES EVEN THOUGH HE HAD ONLY SCRATCHED THEIR SURFACE.

SECOND, HIS OWN SUCCESS IN HIS CHOSEN CAREER WAS DETERMINED BY THE STABILITY OF THE GOLD COAST COLONY AND PROTECTORATE, WHICH IN TURN WAS IN THE HANDS OF SLAVE-OWNING MEN, SOME OF WHOM SAT ON THE JURY. HE KNEW HE HAD TO PLEASE THEM.

STILL, WILLIAM MELTON WAS AT LEAST NOMINALLY AN ABOLITIONIST, AND HE HAD GREAT SYMPATHY, IF NOTHING ELSE, FOR ABINA MANSAH. BUT, IN THE END, THAT WASN'T ENOUGH...

75

PHILOSOPHER AND HISTORIAN MICHEL-ROLPH TROUILLOT SAYS THAT HISTORY IS AN ACT OF SILENCING, IN WHICH THOSE WITHOUT POWER ARE SILENCED AND THOSE WITH POWER ARE ABLE TO SPEAK.

THIS SILENCING TAKES PLACE IN FOUR STAGES:

FIRST, ONLY SOME PERSPECTIVES ON THE PAST ARE EVER RECORDED AS DOCUMENTS. OTHERS--THE PERSPECTIVES OF THE POOR, THE POWERLESS, THE ILLITERATE--ARE NEVER HEARD.

SECOND, ONLY SOME DOCUMENTS EVER MAKE IT TO BE ARCHIVED. OTHERS ARE LOST TO DECAY OR CONSIGNED TO THE TRASH.

THIRD, ONLY SOME ARCHIVED MATERIAL IS EVER TURNED INTO HISTORIES BY HISTORIANS WHO DECIDE WHAT IS IMPORTANT ENOUGH TO WRITE ABOUT, AND WHAT ISN'T.

FINALLY, ONLY SOME HISTORIES ARE CHOSEN BY THE POWERFUL TO BE IN THE CANON, THE LIST OF GREAT BOOKS AND IMPORTANT TOPICS THAT ARE WIDELY READ.

FOLLOWING HER TESTIMONY, THE BOOK WAS CLOSED ON THE STORY OF ABINA MANSAH FOR 125 YEARS. SHE WAS INDEED SILENCED BY HISTORY... AS IF NOBODY HAD HEARD HER AT ALL.

QUAMINA EDDOO APPEARS ONLY INTERMITTENTLY IN THE HISTORICAL RECORDS OF THE TIME, BUT...

...THERE ARE PLENTY OF DOCUMENTS FROM HIS LAWYER JAMES HUTTON BREW, AND EVEN ARTICLES AND BOOKS ABOUT HIM. THE SAME IS TRUE OF WILLIAM MELTON.

MUCH OF THE HISTORY OF THE GOLD COAST IS WRITTEN ABOUT (AND BY) MEN LIKE BREW, AND DAVIS, AND MELTON, FOR THEY ARE IMPORTANT MEN.

BUT NOT ABINA MANSAH. SHE APPEARS IN ONLY ONE PLACE: A DOCUMENT DETAILING THE CASE SHE BROUGHT AGAINST HER MASTER, AND SETTING OUT HER TESTIMONY.

FOR 125 YEARS, HER TESTIMONY WAS HIDDEN ON A SHELF, AND HER VOICE WAS SILENT. BITS OF HER CASE WERE EVEN LOST AT TIMES.

BUT A VOICE LIKE HERS CANNOT BE SILENCED FOREVER, AND ONE DAY, NOT TOO LONG AGO...

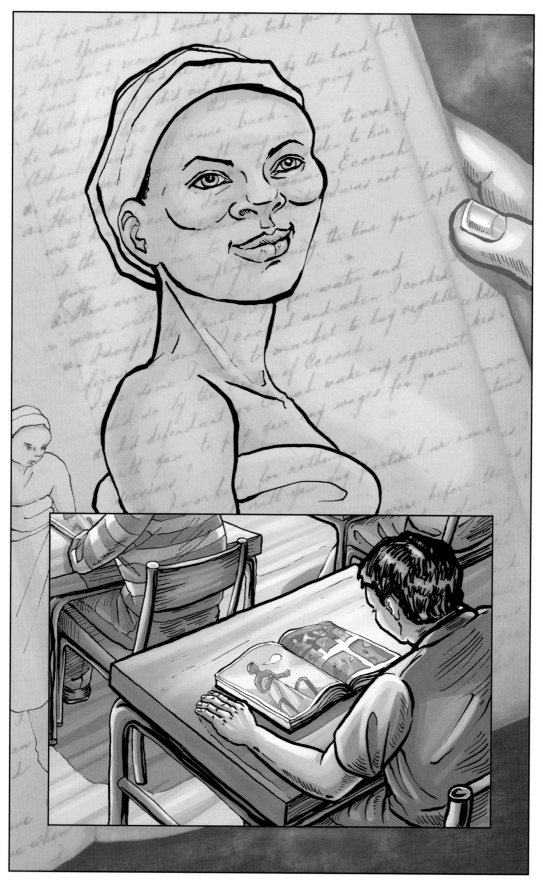

PART II
THE TRANSCRIPT

HYE WON HYE
"THAT WHICH DOES NOT BURN"

SCT 5/4/19 *REGINA V. QUAMINA EDDOO*, 10 NOV 1876

ACTING JUDICIAL ASSESSOR WILLIAM MELTON PRESIDING

Statement of James Davis, Court interpreter

I saw two women who wished to see the Governor. Governor asked why they wished to see him. And they said they were slaves. And the Governor directed me to go with them to the judge to make this statement. One of them called Abinah Mansah stated that she was purchased at a place called Abbedeassi in Adansi and that her master was called Yowahwah, that her master came with her to Salt Pond, and that the master and herself lodged at Quabboo's house: that her master traded with the defendant Quamina Eddoo; that when he made all his purchases he handed her to the defendant Quamina Eddoo sometime in the evening; that on the following morning she went to see her master, but her master had left; that a few days past and Quamina Eddoo said that he had given her as a wife to his slave named Tandoe; and that she declined to be married to Tandoe; that she afterwards heard that she had country people living at Cape Coast; that she ran away to Cape Coast. She was accompanied by her friend and she said that she came to complain because she was purchased; she was sold. (The other Complain-ant said that her master was called Quarbo and had gone up to Ashantee.)

THE TESTIMONY OF ABINA MANSAH

Abinah Mansah, having been promised and declared that she would speak the truth says:

ABINA MANSAH A man called Yowahwah brought me from Ashantee. I was his wife. He brought me to Salt Pond. Yowahwah went on purchasing goods. On the same day as he finished, he handed me over to defendant to be with him, and said that he was going back and would return.

About ten days after the defendant gave me two cloths and told me that he had given me in marriage to one of his house people, and I remonstrated with defendant. I asked him how it was (that when I had been left by Yowah-wah to live with him, and that he would return), that he had given me in marriage to one of his people. On this I thought that I had been sold and I ran away. At the time the defendant said he had given me in marriage to Tan-doe. And the defendant said that if I did not consent to be married to Tandoe he would tie me up and flog me. I heard I had country people living at Cape Coast, and for what the defendant said I ran away and came to Cape Coast.

The defendant's sister said to me "You have taken some cloths to go and wash for some person, but will you not cook for your mother." I thought on this that I had been purchased. That also induced me to run away.

PROSECUTOR DAVIS On the evening as your master took you to the defendant did he say to you "I shall not take away the cloths on your person because I have known your body, but I will cut my beads and did he not cut the beads"?

The form of the question is objected to by Mr. Brew on behalf of the defendant.

PROSECUTOR DAVIS On the evening as your master took you to defendant what did he say to you?

ABINA MANSAH When my master finished buying what he wanted to buy; I carried some of the goods and went with him to his lodgings, and in the evening he handed me to the defendant and said "I should live with the defendant until he returned" that was what he said to me. And after that I thought on what the defendant's sister said to me and I made up my mind to run away as I heard that my country people lived in Cape Coast.

PROSECUTOR DAVIS Anything else?

ABINA MANSAH Nothing else.

ABINA MANSAH When I came to the Court before I said I live at Coo-massie in Ashantee.

PROSECUTOR DAVIS What is read to you now did you not make that statement?

ABINA MANSAH I did make that statement. But two persons called Attah and Sanygar of defendant's house said to me that if I did not consent to be married to Tandoe and live with him they would tie me and flog me. I do not know whether it was the defendant that said so or not.

PROSECUTOR DAVIS That part of your statement where you say that Yawawhah would give you to Quamina Eddoo was it false?

ABINA MANSAH Whether the defendant purchased me or not I do not know. If the defendant had not given me in marriage, I could not have formed any idea that he had purchased me.

PROSECUTOR DAVIS Do you see then that you were a slave?

ABINA MANSAH Yes, I thought I was a slave, because when I went for water or firewood I was not paid.

AJA MELTON When Yawahwah handed you to defendant did defendant receive you? Did he take you by the hand? What did he say?

ABINA MANSAH He (defendant) did not take me by the hand. He [Yawahwah] said "Go live with this man. I am going to Ashantee [Asante] and will come back."

AJA MELTON Were you placed with any woman to work?

ABINA MANSAH He (defendant) gave me to his sister to live with her, because I am a woman. Eccoah is the name of defendant's sister. I was not given to anyone to work.

AJA MELTON How were you employed during the time you were with Eccoah?

ABINA MANSAH I swept the house. I go for water and firewood and I cooked and when I cooked I ate some. I went to market to buy vegetables. I did so by the order of Eccoah.

AJA MELTON Did defendant or Eccoah make any agreement with you to pay you any wages for your services?

ABINA MANSAH No I worked for nothing.

AJA MELTON Did Eccoah call you any particular name?

ABINA MANSAH No

AJA MELTON Did you not say when you were before the court before that she called you her slave?

ABINA MANSAH On the occasion when I went and washed some clothes and returned, defendant's sister said to me: "a person like you go out and wash cloths for other persons not for me nor your master," "did you expect other persons to cook for you to eat," "a slave like you."

AJA MELTON When Eccoah said "Your master" what did she mean?

ABINA MANSAH I cannot answer.

AJA MELTON During the time you were with Eccoah did she compel you to do these things against your will?

ABINA MANSAH In some instances, she said "do so" and "do that" others I did of my own accord.

AJA MELTON When you were a slave at Adansi what kind of work did you do there?

ABINA MANSAH I did the same work as defendant's sister told me.

AJA MELTON When Yowahwah left you with defendant did he take away your cloth?

ABINA MANSAH No only the beads below my knee in remembrance.

AJA MELTON You have been a slave in Adansi and know how slaves are treated, did you experience the same kind of treatment whilst with defendant and his sister?

ABINA MANSAH Yes in the same way that I was treated at Adansi the same way I was treated at Salt Pond.

AJA MELTON Are free persons treated in the same way?

ABINA MANSAH No.

AJA MELTON Then not being treated as a free person what did you consider you were. What did you know that you were?

ABINA MANSAH A slave cannot be treated as a free person. [While] I was a slave at Adansi there is a word by which a person who is a domestic slave and another by which a slave is called which is "Amerperlay" or slave.

AJA MELTON Were you addressed by that name by Eccoah?

ABINA MANSAH On the day that I returned from washing the clothes she called me "Amerperlay" which in the Kreppee means slave.

AJA MELTON Had you a will of your own? Could you do as you pleased without the control of Eccoah?

ABINA MANSAH What came in my own I did it and what came in my own mind I did it.

AJA MELTON Altogether did Eccoah treat you as a free person or as a slave?

ABINA MANSAH She treated me as a slave and called me a slave.

AJA MELTON Did you when she so called and treated you believe that Yowahwah would return?

Here the witness who appears to understand Fantee speaks in that language

ABINA MANSAH I did not think he would return, because Eccoah scolded me and abused me. I thought then that Yowahwah had sold me and that he would not return.

JAMES HUTTON BREW From that time that defendant placed you in his sister's hand did she commence to treat you as a slave?

ABINA MANSAH Yes. When I was handed to Tandoe to be his wife he gave the Handkerchief I hold in my hand. Defendant said he was going to have plenty of cloths sewn for me by this. I thought that I had been sold.

JAMES HUTTON BREW Were you given to Tandoe to be his wife by the defendant without first asking you, without your consent and against your will?

ABINA MANSAH Defendant asked me if I liked him and I said I did not.

JAMES HUTTON BREW Were there any other women in the house of defendant besides yourself?

ABINA MANSAH Yes

JAMES HUTTON BREW Did they do any kind of work also?

ABINA MANSAH Yes

JAMES HUTTON BREW Did they also go for wood and water, marketing and do the same work as you did?

ABINA MANSAH Yes

JAMES HUTTON BREW Were you not aware that all the people in the house were free?

ABINA MANSAH I did not know.

JAMES HUTTON BREW Are you aware that everybody in the Protectorate is freed and that those people you saw in defendant's house are as free as defendant and others?

ABINA MANSAH I did not know that I was free.

JAMES HUTTON BREW As to the others you saw in defendant's house?

ABINA MANSAH I did not know this. They the persons whom I saw are all the children of slaves.

JAMES HUTTON BREW You say you are not aware that all slaves in the Protectorate have been declared free. What led you then to come and lodge this complaint?

ABINA MANSAH I heard that master (meaning white man) had said we were all free. Yet I had been sold and I had no will of my own and I could not look after my body and health: that I am a slave and I would therefore come and complain.

JAMES HUTTON BREW So then you were aware that all the people in defendant's house were free, as you state, with the exception of yourself?

ABINA MANSAH They were not all free, but some were slaves.

JAMES HUTTON BREW [Question repeated.]

ABINA MANSAH I know that all are free.

JAMES HUTTON BREW You said you performed certain work. Were you fed and clothed, if so by whom?

ABINA MANSAH Two cloths were given to me that is all. I was fed by Eccoah.

JAMES HUTTON BREW Did you pay for these and the house you live in?

ABINA MANSAH No

JAMES HUTTON BREW Who put the notion into your head that because you were not paid for the services you rendered you were therefore a slave?

ABINA MANSAH I heard that in this place when a man worked in any way he was paid, but I worked and I was not paid. So I thought I am really purchased.

JAMES HUTTON BREW You heard also that people are fed and clothed for nothing and paid besides for nothing?

ABINA MANSAH I heard that also.

JAMES HUTTON BREW [Question repeated in a different form.]

ABINA MANSAH If one did not work he could not get cloth nor food to eat.

JAMES HUTTON BREW You heard that if you worked you would be fed and clothed and paid altogether?

ABINA MANSAH I heard that.

JAMES HUTTON BREW How long were you in defendant's house before you ran away?

ABINA MANSAH I did not count but I came away in the same month.

JAMES HUTTON BREW Whilst you were there did you see those of whom you have spoken were fed, clothed and paid by defendant?

ABINA MANSAH They had clothes and food given to them. They were not paid.

JAMES HUTTON BREW Were you treated in any way differently from the others or were you all treated alike?

ABINA MANSAH As I was not in the house long I could not tell if he had given them anything before. I did not see him give them anything.

JAMES HUTTON BREW As to treatment.

ABINA MANSAH They were all clothed and fed, but not fed [*sic* . . . meant "paid," I think].

ABINA MANSAH When I came I had two cloths given to me. As they were in defendant's house long before if the defendant had done anything for them I could not tell but as for me he did nothing good for me not having been in the house long, and I ran away.

JAMES HUTTON BREW How were you treated by defendant or his sister that you were induced to run away? Harshly treated by your master the defendant, were you chastised or merely scolded?

ABINA MANSAH I did not live in defendant's house as he gave me to his sister. I lived in his sister's house, if defendant's sister told me to do this and that I got up and went and did it. When I did wrong his sister scolded me but never flogged me.

JAMES HUTTON BREW In going for firewood, water etc. were you compelled to go by any species of coercion or threats or told to do so in the ordinary manner, and you went and did it?

ABINA MANSAH If she says go for firewood, or water or to market I go. She forces me.

JAMES HUTTON BREW Do you mean requested, solicited, or how?

ABINA MANSAH I was asked.

JAMES HUTTON BREW Were you threatened with ill treatment or punishment if you refused to go?

ABINA MANSAH If she said to me "go for firewood" and I said "I won't go," she said if you don't you will be tied and flogged and I said "Now all are free. I also am free. I claim freedom." That was why I ran away.

JAMES HUTTON BREW How often were you threatened with punishment under such circumstances?

ABINA MANSAH About three times.

JAMES HUTTON BREW Was threat of punishment made in the presence of any one besides yourself?

ABINA MANSAH Some children but no elderly person belonging to the house of about from 9 to 13 year of age all girls vis: Accosuah, Abina, Adjuah, Ambah (the eldest of all).

JAMES HUTTON BREW In whose house were these girls living?

ABINA MANSAH In defendant's sister's house.

JAMES HUTTON BREW Is not defendant's sister's house a portion of the house in which defendant lives?

ABINA MANSAH They all lived in one house.

JAMES HUTTON BREW You stated how people were treated as slaves at Adansi. State how slaves and free people are there treated.

ABINA MANSAH At Adansi when a free person is sitting down at ease the slave is working that is what I know.

JAMES HUTTON BREW Did free persons do no work in this household?

ABINA MANSAH On any day when the freeman liked he worked. I did the necessary work such as woman do if it was firewood or water or plantains I went and fetched it.

JAMES HUTTON BREW Were you not cuffed and beaten at times?

ABINA MANSAH I was not long at Adansi before I was brought to this place. When I did wrong I was scolded.

JAMES HUTTON BREW Were you a slave before you came to Adansi?

ABINA MANSAH I was a slave to Eddoo Buffo.

JAMES HUTTON BREW Were you never during that time beaten for misconduct or anything like that?

ABINA MANSAH When I was with Eddo Buffoe and did wrong I was flogged and sometimes I was logged.[1]

JAMES HUTTON BREW Did Eccoah treat you differently to what she did the other maidservants in the house?

ABINA MANSAH She did not treat me in the same manner as she treated those I met in the house. When she gave them cloths she gave me none that is all.

JAMES HUTTON BREW You said that some one threatened to tie her [you?] up and flog her if she would not marry Tandoe. Who was it? Defendant or Seney Agay or Attah?

ABINA MANSAH Attah and Senegay.

JAMES HUTTON BREW You said you made a statement in court in which you declared to as a fact that Yowahwah sold you to defendant. Do you still say so? Of your own knowledge?

ABINA MANSAH If when Yowahwah gave me to defendant to keep, the defendant had not given me in marriage to Tandoe I would not have entertained such an idea that I had been sold. Because defendant gave me in marriage I knew that I had been sold.

JAMES HUTTON BREW In what way were you given in marriage?

ABINA MANSAH My master said that I should be married to Tandoe and that he would give me plenty of cloths, and I said I did not like him. Defendant was in earnest. Tandoe first gave me this handkerchief, but my master was vexed and asked Tandoe why he gave me this when he was going to give me plenty of cloths.

JAMES HUTTON BREW You said that only one occasion Eccoah called you a slave. Did she say "you are my slave" or that "Eddoo's slave" or simply that you are a slave?

---

1 Chained to a log as punishment.

ABINA MANSAH "You are your master's slave." When she said this I sat down and said I did not like this and I made up my mind to come away.

JAMES HUTTON BREW You are certain of this?

ABINA MANSAH Yes Ambah and Adjuah and Accosuah were present.

JAMES HUTTON BREW Do you know how much you were sold for?

ABINA MANSAH I do not know.

JAMES HUTTON BREW Do you know how slaves are sold and handed over?

ABINA MANSAH I know it.

JAMES HUTTON BREW Are any ceremonies observed on such occasions, if so what?

ABINA MANSAH Yes

JAMES HUTTON BREW Were any of them gone through on your alleged sale to Edoo?

ABINA MANSAH There was no observance kept to show the sale of a slave, the only thing which was done was the cutting of the beads at the time.

JAMES HUTTON BREW Is that one of the observances?

ABINA MANSAH It was one.

The Court considering that Mr. Brew has given good and sufficient grounds to the Court that the case be tried by a Jury. Orders accordingly that a Jury be empanelled for Monday next.

THE TESTIMONY OF ECCOAH COOM

ECCOAH COOM, Sworn states: I live at Anamaboe. I am the sister of the defendant and occasionally stay for 2 or 3 days at defendant's house. I have a separate house of my own where I reside.

JAMES DAVIS Did this person (pointing to Abina Mansah) live with you?

ECCOAH COOM I met her at defendant's house and she lived with me.

JAMES DAVIS Did not defendant go out some time ago and do some washing and when she returned what did you say to her?

ECCOAH COOM She did not go out to wash but to fetch water at 6 AM with a brass pan. She returned at 2 o'clock and started the water into a pot and I said to her "You have been starving today. If you knew you would not return soon why did you not take Cankey [Kenkey] to eat with you?" She said "No I was not hungry."

JAMES DAVIS Whilst she was living with you, was it as a stranger?

ECCOAH COOM When I saw her in defendant's house I asked my brother (the defendant) where she came from. He replied some young man of mine brought her. He said she should live with me until he returned when he would go with her. She was living with me as a stranger.

JAMES DAVIS Do you know that the complainant Abina is the slave of your brother, or was purchased by him?

ECCOAH COOM I know that Complainant was not purchased by my brother. She is not the slave of my brother.

ABINA MANSAH When I was living with you did you not tell me to say that when any person asked me, that I belonged to Anomaboe and lived there and that I recently came to live at Salt Pond?

ECCOAH COOM No I did not tell you such a thing.

ABINA MANSAH When some man came and asked you where I came from, did you not say that I came from Anomaboe recently?

ECCOAH COOM I did not.

Question repeated.

ECCOAH COOM No one has come there to ask me such a question.

AJA MELTON Do you know a man called Yowahwah?

ECCOAH COOM No. I have seen him in the Court but never before.

AJA MELTON Did you know where the Complainant came from?

ECCOAH COOM No.

AJA MELTON How long did she stay with you?

ECCOAH COOM I did not reckon.

AJA MELTON How came she to leave you?

ECCOAH COOM I do not know.

AJA MELTON Did you send her for firewood?

ECCOAH COOM No

AJA MELTON How did you treat her, as a guest, a servant or a slave?

ECCOAH COOM She ate together with me.

AJA MELTON Do you never call her a slave?

ECCOAH COOM I do not remember calling her so.

AJA MELTON Did you give her any cloths?

ECCOAH COOM No my brother has given her cloths. When a stranger is living with you and the time is not arrived that he should leave you give him a cloth.

AJA MELTON Do you know a person called Tandoe?

ECCOAH COOM I knew a person called Tandoe, he is dead. He died about 6 months ago[.] [T]here were 2 persons of that name.

AJA MELTON Is there a person called Tandoe in the employ of the defendant?

ECCOAH COOM Yes

AJA MELTON Was he formerly a slave of defendant?

ECCOAH COOM Yes

AJA MELTON Do you know whether defendant gave Complainant to him for a wife?

ECCOAH COOM I do not know

AJA MELTON Did Tandoe ever give her a handkerchief?

ECCOAH COOM I do not know.

AJA MELTON As you are in your brother's house 2 or 3 days at a time do you know the people who came from Ashantee to trade with him?

ECCOAH COOM Sometimes I met some Ashantee traders in the house. I never met Yawahwah. I do not know that he is one of my brother the defendant's boys or traders.

AJA MELTON When defendant gave you Complainant what did he say to you?

ECCOAH COOM He did not give her to me.

AJA MELTON How did she come to live in your house?

ECCOAH COOM My brother placed her in my hands and said when you eat give her some. I knew that she was a stranger. My brother said she was the servant of a friend of his and that he had Complainant to live with him and that when he returned he would go with her.

AJA MELTON Did you ever have occasion to scold the girl?

ECCOAH COOM I never had any. She did nothing wrong to me nor I to her and I never scolded her.

AJA MELTON During the time she staid [sic] with you how did you treat her?

ECCOAH COOM Every morning I cook and eat with her.

AJA MELTON You have several girls living with you as domestics. Were they and Complainant treated in the same way?

ECCOAH COOM Yes.

AJA MELTON Then you treat your servants as you would a guest or stranger?

ECCOAH COOM Yes

AJA MELTON Did you not order Complainant to sweep the house, fetch wood and water, and go to market?

ECCOAH COOM No she did them of her own accord.

JAMES HUTTON BREW Did you ever threaten to punish her if she did not obey your commands in any way?

ECCOAH COOM I never threatened her. I never threatened to chastise her if she did not obey my orders. I state so positively.

JAMES HUTTON BREW Have you never on any occasion called complainant your brother's slave?

ECCOAH COOM No

JAMES HUTTON BREW Did you never term her a slave and treat her as such?

ECCOAH COOM Never

JAMES HUTTON BREW In what way did you treat her harshly or as an ordinary guest?

ECCOAH COOM I did not treat her harshly but as one would treat a stranger.

JAMES HUTTON BREW Now as to the Customs of the Country. Supposing you put up as a stranger in another part of the Country would you not sweep the house; go for wood and water voluntarily?

ECCOAH COOM Yes

JAMES HUTTON BREW Complainant says that you threatened her with punishment on 3 separate occasions if she would not go for wood and water. Did you ever do anything of the kind?

ECCOAH COOM I never did

JAMES HUTTON BREW Did you treat the Complainant as you would have done any other guest who came to live with your brother and who if placed under your special care as in this instance, or in any way as a slave?

ECCOAH COOM Yes as to treating as a guest. I did not treat her like a slave. And that the services Complainant did of going for wood, water etc she did of her own accord without any coercion of any kind.

Adjourned until Monday morning 11 AM 13 November 1876.

It being impossible to get the jurors to attend on Monday the case Resumed on Tuesday 14th November 1876

Eleven jurors appear and were sworn. The evidence as taken in the foregoing pages was read to the Jury by the Clerk of the Court

THE TESTIMONY OF ADJUAH N'YAMIWHAH

ADJUAH N'YAMIWHAH, *Having promised and declared that she could speak the truth says.* I now live in Cape Coast. I was a slave at Ashantee and was bought to Salt Pond about a month ago. I know Abina Mansah. I knew her in Ashantee and when we came to Salt Pond we lived together. I was brought to Salt Pond before she was brought. I saw Abina Mansah brought to Salt Pond by Yowahwah.

We lived together at one house at first we had our meals. Sometime in the evening Yowahwah came and called the Complainant. The Complainant did not return. I saw Yowahwah. I asked him where the Complainant was. He said she was in her Master's house and that he had sold her to Quamina Eddoo (the defendant).

On the following day I went to see Complainant. I saw her and asked her why she had not come to see us and whether that the house in which I saw her was the house to which she was brought. She replied "yes"! And as to the question why did she not come to see us, she said she was doing something and that she was busy, and that Yowahwah had sold her and had gone away and that she did not see him. I left the Complainant.

Some time after that I cooked my meals. I went and called her, she came and partook of some with me.

JAMES DAVIS When Yowahwah brought the Complainant did you and Yawahwah and Complainant live together in one house?

ADJUAH N'YAMIWHAH Yes

JAMES DAVIS What was Abina Mansah to Yowahwah?

ADJUAH N'YAMIWHAH She was a wife to Yowahwah

JAMES DAVIS How many days after their arrival did Yowahwah tell you that he had sold Abina Mansah?

ADJUAH N'YAMIWHAH They arrived on Monday. On the same day he sold her. On the following day he purchased his goods. On the next day he left.

JAMES DAVIS Did you ask Yowahwah to whom he sold Complainant?

ADJUAH N'YAMIWHAH I asked him, and he said he had sold her to Quamina Eddoo and that Quamina Eddoo was her master.

JAMES DAVIS Did you ask him why he had sold her, she being his wife?

ADJUAH N'YAMIWHAH I asked him. He made no reply.

JAMES DAVIS Did Yowahwah say to you afterwards that if Abina Mansah came, you should say to her that he had bidden her goodbye?

ADJUAH N'YAMIWHAH He said nothing of the kind.

JAMES DAVIS Then you knew that Yowahwah bought his wife and he had sold her?

ADJUAH N'YAMIWHAH Yes.

JAMES DAVIS And you say that Complainant said to you that her master said to you when he came to you that her master had sold her?

ADJUAH N'YAMIWHAH When she came to me she was crying and said her husband had sold her and gone away to Ashantee.

JAMES DAVIS Then you knew that your friend had been sold and joined your Company?

ADJUAH N'YAMIWHAH Yes

No further questions

AJA MELTON What was the condition of Ambah [*sic*] Mansah at Ashantee?

ADJUAH N'YAMIWHAH She was formerly the slave to Eddoo Buffoo. I saw her living in a state of slavery in his hands.

AJA MELTON What was the reason of being brought down to Salt Pond?

ADJUAH N'YAMIWHAH Kofi Calcally the ex king of Ashantee, caught and sold her to Yowahwah. She was caught at Quawnoomah. I was present. I was also present when Yowahwah bought her from Kofi Calcally and Yawahwah brought her to Salt Pond. When Abina Mansah came with her master she lived in Quabo's house. I was staying in Quaboe's house.

AJA MELTON When did Abina Mansah become the wife of Yowahwah. Before he purchased her or afterwards?

ADJUAH N'YAMIWHAH He married her after he bought her. He took her after he purchased her.

AJA MELTON Did he purchase her as a wife or as a slave?

ADJUAH N'YAMIWHAH As a wife but he had her as a slave also when he purchased her he said [s]he was his wife. Then he made her a slave, brought her to Salt Pond and sold her.

AJA MELTON Did you see anything of Abina Mansah after Yowahwah left?

ADJUAH N'YAMIWHAH Yes at the defendant's house. She went for firewood and water and swept the house. Abina Mansah lived with Eccoah. Yawahwah sold her to Quamina Eddoo (the defendant). Complainant told me that Quamina Eddoo said that she Abina Mansah was to live with his sister Eccoah.

JAMES HUTTON BREW Do you know what is the truth?

ADJUAH N'YAMIWHAH Yes it is to state what I have seen.

JAMES HUTTON BREW Where was Abina Mansah sold to Yawahwah?

ADJUAH N'YAMIWHAH At Quawnoomah

JAMES HUTTON BREW At the same place where she was caught?

ADJUAH N'YAMIWHAH When she was caught there, she was sold there.

JAMES HUTTON BREW And King Calcarry was there?

ADJUAH N'YAMIWHAH Yes. He was at Quanoomah

JAMES HUTTON BREW And you and Abina and Yowahwah and Kofi Calcarry were all in the same house?

ADJUAH N'YAMIWHAH Yowahwah came from Adansi and purchased Abinah. We three were in one house.

JAMES HUTTON BREW And the bargain was made and struck by the king in your own presence?

ADJUAH N'YAMIWHAH Yes

JAMES HUTTON BREW What was the figure?

ADJUAH N'YAMIWHAH In Ashantee they do not sell a person when many persons are present. When the seller and purchaser have finished talking then the buyer goes and fetches the slave.

JAMES HUTTON BREW Then you were not present when the bargain was struck!

ADJUAH N'YAMIWHAH I was not present, but I saw that she was taken away by Yawahwah.

JAMES HUTTON BREW Now were you present, or not present?

ADJUAH N'YAMIWHAH It is not usual for a woman to be present. I was not present.

JAMES HUTTON BREW On what day did Yowahwah arrive at Salt Pond?

ADJUAH N'YAMIWHAH On a Monday

JAMES HUTTON BREW On what day did he sell Abina as you state?

ADJUAH N'YAMIWHAH On the same Monday. In the evening we went to the street and took her to Quamina Eddoo's house.

JAMES HUTTON BREW On what day did Yowahwah make his purchases as stated by you?

ADJUAH N'YAMIWHAH On Tuesday. On Wednesday he left.

JAMES HUTTON BREW Then Yowahwah sold Abinah before he made his purchases?

ADJUAH N'YAMIWHAH. Yes. I am speaking the truth. Abinah did not carry any of the goods. I am certain of that.

JAMES HUTTON BREW Abina stated that he purchased the goods and she carried them and that she was afterwards sold. Which is the correct statement?

ADJUAH N'YAMIWHAH When he went and sold Abina on the evening of the Monday, on Tuesday he made his purchases, on Wednesday he left for Ashantee. When he purchased the goods Abinah did not carry any. What I am stating is the truth.

JAMES HUTTON BREW Which statement is true, yours or Abinah's?

ADJUAH N'YAMIWHAH Mine.

THE TESTIMONY OF YOWAHWAH

Witnesses for the defense **YOWAHWAH** *Having promised and declared that he would speak the truth says* I come from Adanse and am a trader.

JAMES HUTTON BREW Do you know Abinah Mansah?

YOWAHWAH I know her. She is my wife.

JAMES HUTTON BREW Do you know Quamina Eddoo (defendant)?

YOWAHWAH I do

JAMES HUTTON BREW Where did you first know him?

YOWAHWAH At Salt Pond. I have been there about 10 times to trade.

JAMES HUTTON BREW Did you go to any house in particular to trade?

YOWAHWAH Yes it was defendant Quamina Eddoo's house where I always lived.

JAMES HUTTON BREW When you last [were] at Salt Pond at whose house did you put up?

YOWAHWAH When I went this last time Quamina Eddoo's house was full of traders and he said go and lived [*sic*] in one of my young men's house—Quarboes' house.

JAMES HUTTON BREW After this did you go back to defendant's house again and at any time while you were at Salt Pond?

YOWAHWAH I did. I went there with my wife because I received a message from a place called Thessoo in Assin that my brother who lived there was dangerously ill and dying and that I should make haste and go to see him before he died, and when I went to defendant I told him and said that I would leave my wife with him until I went to see my brother and returned. I bought nothing. I went away empty. I found that my brother had died and I went to inform my relatives at Ashantee.

JAMES HUTTON BREW Are we to understand that you left your wife Abina the Complainant in the care of the defendant at Salt Pond until his return from Thessoo under the circumstances just stated and that he [you?] parted with her from in no other way or manner whatsoever?

YOWAHWAH Exactly so.

JAMES HUTTON BREW You know the last witness?

YOWAHWAH Yes.

JAMES HUTTON BREW Now she stated that you told her you had sold Abinah to defendant. Is this true?

YOWAHWAH I never made any such statement to her.

JAMES HUTTON BREW Did you not tell her that you had sold Abinah and that she was in defendant's house at Salt Pond?

YOWAHWAH I did not.

JAMES HUTTON BREW The last witness said that she met you and Abinah at Salt Pond and that you purchased goods the day after you sold Abinah. Is that statement true?

YOWAHWAH It is not true. I purchased no goods.

JAMES HUTTON BREW When last witness she asked you why you had sold your wife she said you said nothing. Is that true?

YOWAHWAH No! She asked me a question[. I]f I wanted to sell my wife I would not have come to this place to sell her.

JAMES HUTTON BREW In what way did you hand her over to Quamina Eddoo as a slave or what?

YOWAHWAH I left her with defendant and said to him "Friend this is my wife," "I leave her with you" "Take care of her for me" "When I return I will take my wife away with me." This I said in the presence of my wife and Be-prah.

JAMES HUTTON BREW Did you not take off her wife's cloth and cut off her beads and the like before handing over to Eddoo?

YOWAHWAH No

ABINA MANSAH Did you not say that you were taking away the beads I had on my leg and I said to you "I am your wife. You say you left me with Eddoo to take care of me and you would return, [so] how is it you are going to cut off my beads?" and you said that you were going to take the beads with you in remembrance.

YOWAHWAH I did not say so to you.

ABINA MANSAH When you took me to Eddoo I asked you whether you had brought me to sell me and you said "Yes" and you also said "bye and bye when I return" I shall have some cloth for you to wear. Was this so?

YOWAHWAH This was not so, it is a false accusation.

ABINA MANSAH On the night when you went and left me with Eddoo did you call me to sleep with you?

YOWAHWAH No

ABINA MANSAH Did you take your leave of me saying Yaw would return?

YOWAHWAH I did so when I left you with Eddoo.

Complainant says that this is false and that witness cannot dare say that he did not sell me. I have no more questions but he has sold me.

JAMES DAVIS When the message that your brother was sick [arrived] was Abina present?

YOWAHWAH She was. If I had sold Complainant, when I was invited to come here I would not come.

JAMES DAVIS The Complainant being your wife as you said and you left her with the defendant, did you leave any small amount of money with her for subsistence until you returned?

YOWAHWAH I left it with the defendant and said to him that my wife did not understand buying with silver money[. K]eep this money for her subsistence till I return and I will take away my wife.

JAMES DAVIS Did you leave her with defendant as your master or your friend?

YOWAHWAH My master (as we usually call a person).

JAMES DAVIS Did you not sell her?

YOWAHWAH No.

AJA MELTON How did you get possessed of Abina whom you call your wife?

YOWAHWAH By paying head-sum for her. I paid 1 oz [gold] for her to an elderly relative of mine named Fourie about 10 months ago at Edoobiassie in Adansi.

AJA MELTON Did you hear of your wife as you call her being given to another man at Salt Pond?

YOWAHWAH I have not heard it.

AJA MELTON Did you know Quacoe Dabrah at Quawnoomah?

YOWAHWAH No I have not been to that place.

ABINA MANSAH *recalled by court*

AJA MELTON Have you heard what the witness has said as to how he became possessed of you as a wife[?] You have said all along that he purchased you and sold you. Which statement is the Court to believe?

ABINA MANSAH My statement is the true one.

The jury are unanimously of opinion that the Defendant in the above case is not guilty of any of the charges specified in the Indictment.—D. Mac-Kenzie, Foreman

Verdict, Not Guilty: W. Melton, Acting Judicial Assessor, Court House, Cape Coast, 14 November, 1876

PART III
HISTORICAL CONTEXT

NKYIMU
"PRECISION IS NECESSARY"

In the previous two sections of this book, you have encountered a **primary source** and a **secondary source**. The primary source (Part II) is a document from the nineteenth century that purports to be an eyewitness description of what happened in the courtroom in which Abina Mansah appeared in 1876 and which contains an account of her life up to that point. The secondary source (Part I) is a graphic interpretation of that document jointly prepared by a historian and an artist. Like many others who interpret the past, we have strived to create a representation that is reasonably accurate, authentic to the experiences and perspectives of the individuals represented, and useful to our audience. How did we turn the short primary source into a longer interpretation that tried to meet these criteria? How can we know whether our account of the events surrounding Abina Mansah's day in court is a reasonably accurate and useful interpretation? How can you, the reader, trust the work we have produced?

In the next three parts of this book, we will attempt to answer those questions by sharing with you the process we went through in developing our interpretation. We will show you the information we used and discuss the questions we asked ourselves as we wrote and illustrated Abina's story. The first task in this process is to explain our understanding of the time and place in which Abina and the "important men" lived (Part III). Then, we will also share with you the philosophical, ethical, and theoretical questions that confronted us and our solutions for dealing with them (Part IV). Finally, we will discuss the response to the first edition of the book and explore some new interpretations that have resulted from the author's and illustrator's interactions with scholars, students, and the public (Part V).

The act of setting a historical narrative in the context of the time and place in which it happened is called **historicization**. Most historians see their job as reconstructing past events. They seek to understand not only what happened but also how people experienced events and why these events happened. Like detectives, historians work with evidence—written documents, archaeological remains, spoken words—each of which provides only a small part of the story. Only by putting these small parts together can historians get a reasonable understanding of what happened, why it happened, and how people who lived in that time and place experienced it. For *Abina and the Important Men*, that means gaining a better understanding of what life was like on the Gold Coast in 1876, of the institution of slavery and its abolition in the region, and finally, of the biographies of the main individuals in the story.

THE GOLD COAST, CA. 1876

The **Gold Coast** is a name bestowed by Europeans upon a stretch of West Africa roughly approximating the southern half of the modern-day state of Ghana (see Map 1). The name derives from the fact that from the eighth to the sixteenth century (and even today) the inhabitants of the region extracted a great deal of gold that entered the world economy, first by crossing the Sahara Desert into North Africa, and later, through trade with European merchants who visited the coast. In fact, gold was only one of many materials in this region's history produced by the hard work of its people and from its rich soil and desired by the outside world. Over the past millennium, both waves of foreigners and the local population have sought their wealth from the soil and people of the Gold Coast, whether by trading in gold, kola nuts, palm oil, or cocoa.

EARLY HISTORY

The human presence in West Africa stretches back many thousands of years, but for most of that period the Gold Coast was populated by many small bands of hunter-gatherers. Traces of their language may survive in the Etsi or Guan languages still spoken by a few groups along the coast and in the mountains of the region today. However, recent research suggests that agriculture became prevalent in the savanna to the north as far back as ca. 1700 B.C.E., and over the next two millennia foraging slowly gave way to a more settled way of life in the forest zone of the Gold Coast, where first yams, and later cassava and plantains, became the staple foods of dense populations.

In the fifteenth century (ca. 1440 C.E.), the period from which emerge the oldest surviving written sources for the forest region that we know as the Gold Coast, large-scale, organized societies that subsisted on agriculture—and which produced enough of a surplus to support a specialized labor force—developed. The people in these societies spoke languages that later developed into the modern languages of southern Ghana—Ga-Adangbe, Ewe, and especially the **Akan** family of Twi languages (Fante, Akuapem,

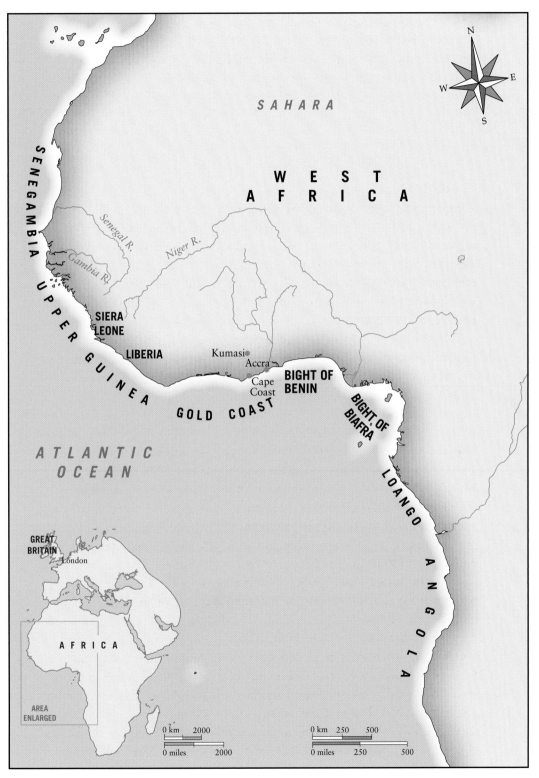

MAP 1 West Africa and the Gold Coast

and **Asante**) (see Map 2). It was the Twi-speaking Akan people who came to dominate the area discussed in this story. Like many of their neighbors, the Akan organized themselves over several centuries into a society that had several major institutions. The most important of these was and remains the *abusua*, or extended family (see Glossary). The abusua institution probably developed in order to organize shared family labor for big tasks like clearing forests to plant crops, and also in order to promote the fertility of the community. The abusua was a way for a large group to provide resources to members in need, especially childbearing women and also children. These large-scale groups were (and remain) largely organized along the lines of **matrilineality**. In other words, every individual is a member of a particular abusua through his or her mother and not his or her father. In fact, however, abusua membership is often assimilative, with people being brought in from outside the group as members. In fact, one feature of *slavery* in the region in the eighteenth and early nineteenth centuries was the assimilation of captives into full membership of the abusua.

In addition to the abusua, Akan societies also developed the **oman** (plural: *aman*), or states ruled by chiefs and kings chosen from within leading abusua. The chief, or **ohene** (plural: *ahenfo*) of an oman could often exercise a great deal of power, but his actions usually were also monitored, and sometimes overturned, by leading men and women of the community who served as advisors, judges, priests, and even legislators.

From at least the seventeenth century, as well, the common people of the community found a way to participate in the politics of the community and the oman through the development of the *asafo*. These brotherhoods (and possibly sisterhoods) organized people into groups for community labor, defense, firefighting, and other tasks, but they also came to play a role in politics by sometimes opposing the power of the chiefs. In short, Akan society was organized into states, families, and brotherhoods. The people did not live in *tribes*, a term commonly misapplied to the region. Nor were the chiefs arbitrary or despotic rulers. Rather, their power was checked by institutions that represented different classes and communities.

SOCIETAL AND POLITICAL CHANGES: ASANTE AND THE EUROPEANS

Two important changes after the sixteenth century complicated Akan society. The first was the rise of the state of Asante (sometimes called Ashanti) around 1700. Centered several hundred miles north of the coastline, Asante began as a confederation of allied aman whose leading families organized for self-defense but whose armies soon defeated many surrounding states

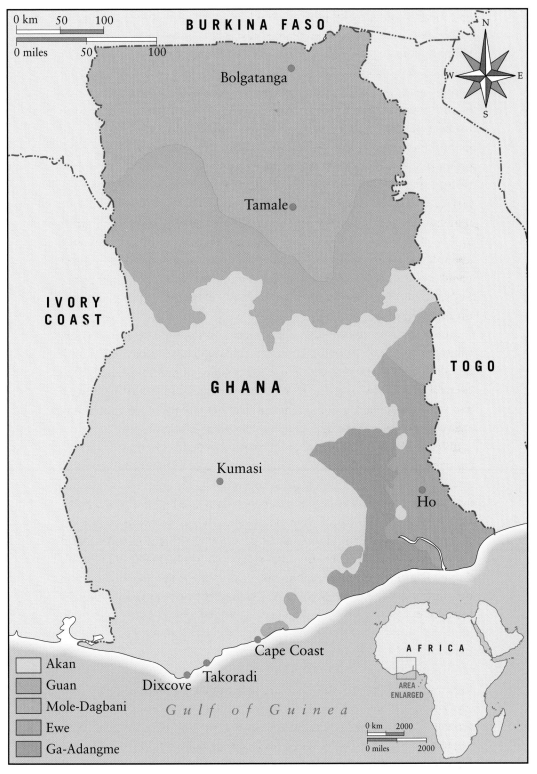

MAP 2 Major Language Groups of Ghana

and slowly grew to control the valuable gold and kola trades in the region. Later, they also became a powerful force in the slave trade. By the late eighteenth century, the Asante Confederation was organized under a single ruling abusua and it loosely controlled the zone extending from the coast to deep into the interior—roughly the same area as the state of Ghana today (see Map 3).

The other important political change of this period was the emergence of Europeans as political players on the coast. Portuguese merchants had arrived in the region as early as 1471 with charters from their king to pursue the trade in gold. They quickly made an alliance with the rulers of the town of Elmina, close to Cape Coast. They were followed by the Dutch in the 1590s, and soon after the English, French, Danish, Swedish, and even German traders. However, for several centuries local rulers were able to play these Europeans off of each other and effectively limit their political reach.

This balance of power changed around the mid-nineteenth century. First, the development of new technologies and medicines, such as steamships and quinine, allowed the Europeans to pursue military and political power further into the interior. Second, the Industrial Revolution enabled Britain in particular to enlarge its military and commercial power to the point that it was able to eventually drive the other European powers out of the region, with the Danish (1850) and Dutch (1871–1872) being the last to leave. Finally, the emergence of palm oil as a strategic resource for the British led them to invest more energy and effort in controlling the region. Palm oil was useful for two major industrial needs—as machine lubricant and in the production of soap.

The main challenge the British faced was the regional supremacy of the Asante state. Ruling over the principal palm oil–producing regions and the major ports of the area, the Asante kings seemed unchallengeable. Fortunately for the British, however, the rulers (ahenfo) of some states (aman), including the kings of the coastal town of Cape Coast and their nearby allies, resented Asante power and were willing to assist them. In the 1850s and 1860s, a series of conflicts broke out between the Asante and their allies on the one hand and a British-led coalition on the other. This coalition included the Fante Confederation, a traditional alliance of states in the area around Cape Coast. In the 1860s and 1870s, the leaders of this Confederation sought independence from Asante as an independent state allied with Britain. In 1873, the British crown sent a major force to the region and, along with Fante forces and other local allies, pushed the Asante back from the coast.

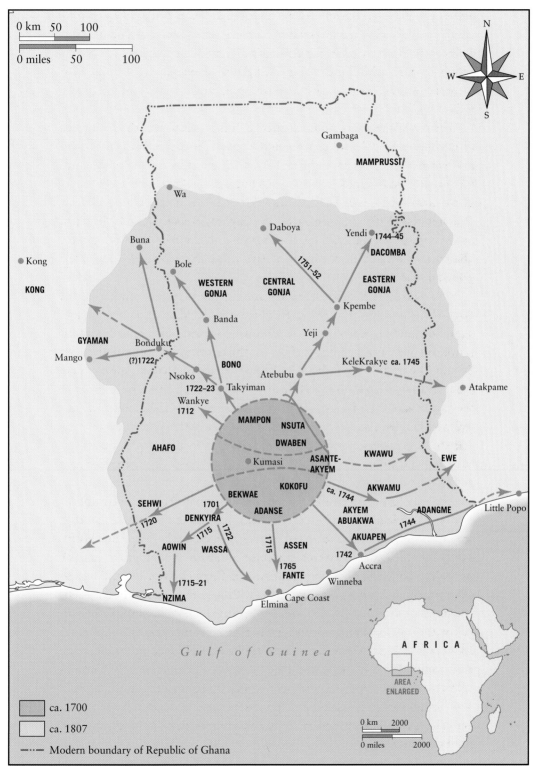

MAP 3 The Expansion of the Asante Kingdom, ca. 1700–1807

Out of the chaos left by the Asante retreat, the British managed to create a system of agreements with local rulers that was formalized in the creation of a *Colony* and a *Protectorate*. The **Colony**, where it was generally accepted that the British ruled formally, was legally limited to a few large towns like Cape Coast, which could be controlled by the large forts that had served for generations as defensive establishments and for holding slaves. The bulk of the region became the **Protectorate**, which included the small and large states that had supported Britain in the 1873–1874 war as well as others who had been Asante allies but were now controlled by ahenfo sympathetic to British rule. Technically, these states were independent. Nevertheless, they had to accept certain rules imposed by the British including, technically, the abolition of all slavery.

THE BRITISH CIVILIZING MISSION

That the British were, by the late eighteenth century, the biggest proponents of the abolition of slavery worldwide was something of an irony, since they had in previous centuries been the world's largest slave dealers. This switch from slave trading to abolitionism in Britain in the nineteenth century reflected wider changes in British society. The Industrial Revolution that had begun in the eighteenth century had created a new middle-class society of industrialists, financiers, and even shop owners in Britain who were wealthy but largely lacked the political clout of the old aristocracy. This class helped to fund a community of enlightenment thinkers who developed a concept of liberalism. These new ideas celebrated the hard work and free market economy of the middle class, and allowed them to represent these values as more virtuous than those of the aristocrats, many of whom were slave owners. It was a religious as well as secular ideology, including the notion of *evangelizing*, or convincing others to live according to their values. It was also a useful political ideology, allowing the middle class to see themselves as more deserving of governing the country than the upper classes whom they were seeking to replace. In the late eighteenth century, the British middle class turned this ideology upon their own working classes as a sort of propaganda campaign, trying to convince them to support the middle classes and to aspire to live like them.

This internal campaign became international in the early nineteenth century as members of the British middle class arrived at the notion that they were not only the superior class in society, but also as a nation the most "civilized" people of the world. Thus the duty to convince the lower classes to envy and support the middle classes in Britain morphed into the concept that the British had a duty to bring their values and "civilization" to everyone else. This "civilization" included Christian evangelism, a belief in free trade and free labor rather than slavery, and support for democratic ideals. It was a powerful set of ideals that found expression in the famous words of one of the great architects of the empire, Joseph Chamberlain:

> We feel now that our rule over these territories can only be justified if we can show that it adds to the happiness and prosperity of the people, and I maintain that our rule does, and has, brought security and peace and comparative prosperity to countries that never knew these blessings before. In carrying out this work of civilization we are fulfilling what I believe to be our national mission, and we are finding scope for the exercise of these faculties and qualities which have made of us a great governing race . . . in almost every instance in which the rule of the Queen has been established . . . there has come with it greater security to life and property, and a material improvement in the condition of the bulk of the population. (Speech to the Royal Colonial Institute, London, March 31, 1897)

Were the British justified in believing that they were more civilized than others, and that they therefore had a right to force or cajole other people to live in ways acceptable to the British middle class? Ironically, while the civilizing mission included a message of "democracy" and freedom, it also found ways to depict Africans and others as being unworthy of self-rule and self-determination. In Britain, the new enlightenment ideology had excluded certain groups—children, those deemed insane or criminal, and women, for example—from enjoying equality. Instead, these groups were to be "protected" and watched over by the male head of household or the British state, which was seen as sort of a national father figure. This masculine ideal is described further in the section on gender in Part V.

By the mid-nineteenth century, similar language was being applied in the colonies, where Africans, South Asians, and others were spoken of as being "childlike," "savages," or "feminine" and thus unworthy of full participation or rights. By the 1870s, when Abina lived, these ideas were supported by a pseudoscientific language of racism that sought to scientifically justify their permanent exclusion from rights and thus Britain's rule of the colonies. At the same time, however, it must be recognized that many British administrators, missionaries, and others still truly *believed* that they were acting in the best interests of their African "wards."

THE CIVILIZING MISSION IN THE GOLD COAST

Within the Gold Coast, this sense was reflected partly in the drive by British administrators to try to reorganize local communities along the lines of British, middle-class society. This was especially pronounced in the Colony and specifically the town of Cape Coast. Once ruled by the larger oman of Fetu, Cape Coast had achieved its independence in the eighteenth century by exploiting the wealth of its merchants earned through trade with Europeans. But this self-rule was short-lived, as first Asante and later Britain came to claim the town. The British sought to impose new rules on the city, including British-style housing, straight roads, new decision-making bodies, and rules about what behavior was acceptable in the city. In order to pay for these projects, they tried to raise revenues through taxation. The rulers of Cape Coast did not always accept these measures without protest. In 1844, the leading *asafo* signed a protest against a British tax. Then in 1865 John Aggrey, the king of Oguaa (the Fante state in which Cape Coast was located) got into a conflict with the British administrator over who had the right to imprison criminals. As a result, the British replaced him, ignoring the widespread protests that resulted.

Despite these conflicts, Europeans and Africans interacted relatively freely in the town on a day-to-day basis. By the 1870s Cape Coast contained a large population of English-speaking Africans and Euro-Africans of mixed heritage. Many of these individuals formed a class of professionals and merchants who were generally supportive of British attitudes, traded and worked with the British administrators and commercial companies, and saw themselves as at least partly British in identity. It was these men who tried to create European-style but independent states such as the Accra Confederation and who wrote a constitution for the Fante Confederation of 1873. Many of their attitudes were reflected in newspapers meant to serve these English-speaking West Africans, like the *African Times*, whose Sierra Leonean editor in 1872 described himself as follows:

> A strenuous upholder of British influence and rule on the West coast of Africa as being the only one possible under which the spread of civilization and Christianity, and a large development of material resources, could ever be effected. (*African Times*, February 28, 1872, p. 94)

However, such attitudes did not necessarily extend to the lower classes of Cape Coast, and even less so to the population of the Protectorate territories beyond its walls. Even the greatest supporters of British "civilization" often resented the realities of British rule, and administrators faced opposition to many of their actions throughout this era.

SLAVERY IN THE GOLD COAST

In the mid-1870s, an appreciable proportion of that Protectorate population was made up of people whom we can call *slaves*, although that label is somewhat imprecise, as we discuss in Part V of this volume. A more accurate picture of enslavement in the region must include a historical account that ties it to the history and societies of the region.

Through written, oral, and archaeological sources we know that the Akan and their neighbors had developed a variety of social statuses in the period leading up to the sixteenth century. These can be understood partly by looking again at the various institutions of their societies. For example, individuals' identities and access to resources were tied to their membership in an extended family (abusua). What happened to people who were kicked out of their abusua for crimes or transgressions, or whose abusua broke apart due to famine or warfare? Such individuals frequently came to be attached to new abusua, but often without the rights and privileges of regular members. Although they might carry out the same types of labor as full members of the family, they did not enjoy the same social status or protections, and certainly not the same ability to move around. These individuals might therefore be called *slaves* with some accuracy.

Similarly, the fact that ahenfo—chiefs—and other leading men were limited in their power by a web of elders and family obligations meant that if they wished to exert their own personal power, they had to find helpers and dependents who were not loyal to any single abusua but rather to them personally. One way to accomplish this was to create a class of "royal slaves." These individuals had become slaves through the breakup of their families or through warfare and kidnapping, and thus were at the bottom of the social ladder. Yet once they came to serve a chief they often could become quite powerful as warriors, bureaucrats, and advisors. Nevertheless, they too were dependent upon the chiefs and had restricted rights.

In fact, most everyone in Akan society was tied to other people through a network of obligations, and many of these relationships were somehow uneven. These obligations are often described as *ako-awura* relationships, a term that could be translated as servant-master or client-patron. These included the relationships between chiefs and their subjects, *asafo* leaders and their followers, family elders and junior members, apprentices and masters, debtors (*awowa*) and those to whom they were indebted. Almost everyone was someone's servant or client (*akoa*) in some way, and even the powerful were servants of the state ruler. Within this thick matrix of relationships, that of the domestic slave, *odonko*, and the master was extreme but not entirely out of line with other statuses.

Several further observations can be made about the institution of the domestic slave in Akan society. First, in contrast to plantation slavery in the Americas, Akan "slavery" was not necessarily or primarily economic, but rather political and social. Slaves may have worked as agricultural laborers and gold miners, but they usually did so alongside the families and individuals to whom they belonged. Second, slavery of this sort remained very limited until the late seventeenth century. Finally, slavery in the Gold Coast was generally assimilative, in that the enslaved could often become full members of the society—and even family—in which they lived over the course of their lives or perhaps a few generations.

THE ATLANTIC SLAVE TRADE AND ABOLITION

The Atlantic slave trade changed this situation gradually but dramatically. We can begin to trace these changes to the seventeenth century, for although some inhabitants of the region were enslaved and carried to the Americas as early as the 1500s, it was not until the 1670s that Europeans really saw the Gold Coast as a place to obtain slaves. Around that date—the height of sugar demand in Europe—Europeans became willing to pay very high prices for African laborers to work in the sugar plantations of Brazil, Louisiana, and the Caribbean. As a result, individuals in the Gold Coast willing to provide European slavers with captives could reap enormous profits. By the 1790s, European and American slave traders were embarking about 74,000 enslaved Africans per year from the region. Some large states, like Asante, became key providers of captives. Many of these captives were obtained from deep in the interior, where Asante armies captured entire communities and forced weaker states to provide enslaved youths as tribute to the Asante crown. In their greed, some chiefs and other Africans also changed the laws and norms of their societies to find ways to sell their own people as slaves. Such "crimes" as defaulting on a debt or committing adultery became punishable by enslavement and sale in some cases. At the same time, European and American ideas of slavery as a permanent institution became prevalent in the Gold Coast, especially as some coastal Africans began to use slaves to produce grain, palm oil, and other products on large farms for sale to Europeans.

Most of the Africans sold into the Atlantic slave trade from this region were men. Not only did American buyers prefer males, but also powerful Africans preferred to retain women (whom they perceived as harder workers and potential wives) within their societies. Thus slavery came more and more to be a "female" condition in the region. When the British banned the slave trade in 1807, and later criminalized slavery in the newly created Colony and Protectorate in 1874, this trend increased. There were several reasons for this, but the main one was that women were seen as being less able to run away or to report their masters and mistresses to the British. We discuss the importance of this feminization of slavery upon Abina's story in Part V.

In fact, most British administrators were uninterested in truly eliminating slavery in the region. Although many of them can be loosely called abolitionists, they were in reality opposed to actively rooting out slavery for several reasons. First, they recognized that the wealth of the colony and its political stability relied on their alliance with local men who were slave owners, and did not wish to alienate this class. Second, they feared that actively liberating enslaved people would cause chaos, which they wished to avoid. Finally, they convinced themselves that slavery in the region was "not that bad" and more like a parent-child relationship than plantation slavery in the Americas.

As a result, the laws banning slavery that came into effect in 1875 technically made it possible for any slave to liberate himself or herself, but did not call for British administrators to actively pursue slave owners or free slaves. This outcome placed the burden on the enslaved to go through a number of difficult steps to liberate himself or herself, slowing down the process of emancipation immensely. It also led to the perception among slave owners that adults, especially men, would make bad slaves since they were most likely to be able to run away, go to court, or otherwise escape. Thus, after 1875, more and more children, especially girls, were enslaved outside the Colony and Protectorate and brought in to serve as slaves.

For these young Africans, achieving liberation was a difficult process. It entailed running away to a society about which they knew very little and where they knew few people, searching out a British magistrate or some other protector who probably cared little about them and whose life and viewpoints were unintelligible, and somehow obtaining their aid. That some of them still managed to do so is an incredible story.

ABINA MANSAH AND THE IMPORTANT MEN

Abina Mansah was one of these young girls. From her testimony, we know quite a bit about her life before she became the "property" of Quamina Eddoo. She was probably born in the eastern Gold Coast, whose majority population were Ewe speakers rather than the Twi-speaking Akan. We know those both because she uses the Ewe term for domestic slave (*amerflefle*, in the testimony written as "amerperlay") and because she tells us that she was first captured by the Asante general Adu Bofo, who invaded the Ewe-speaking region in 1869. However, the only names we have for her are Akan: Abina/Abena, indicating that she was born on a Tuesday, and Mansah/Mensa, that she was a third-born daughter. Thus there is conflicting evidence as to whether she grew up primarily speaking Ewe or Twi.

As a captive, Abina was taken to Asante territory, where she appears to have labored as a domestic slave at two residences. The first was in the capital city of Coomassie [Kumasi], and the second was in the Asante peripheral province of Adansi, which bordered the independent states of the southern Gold Coast that were at the time allied with Britain (see Map 4). Abina then got caught up in a second war, the Anglo-Asante War of 1873–1874, at the end of which she was again taken as spoils of war. This time her captor was the former king of Asante, Kofi Karikari, who had lost his stool (throne) at the end of the war. Karikari then took Abina, along with other captives, to the Asante district of Kwanwoma.

Abina remained in Kwanwoma only for a short time before being purchased by a trader named Yowahwah [Yaw Awoah] who allegedly married her, although possibly this marriage was just a cover to enable him to bring her into the Gold Coast Colony and Protectorate, where slavery was illegal. Abina accompanied Yaw to the town of Salt Pond, not far from Cape Coast and legally within the borders of the Colony. In Salt Pond, Yowahwah then appears to have secretly sold her to Quamina Eddoo, who turned her over to his sister Eccoah. After several weeks, she was told that she was to marry Tandoe, at which point she ran away to her "country-people" in Cape Coast—probably others from the region of Asante in which she had been born. They in turn led her to Davis, who helped her to appear before the court.

Most of this story revolves around Abina's relationship to four important men—Quamina Eddoo, William Melton, James Davis, and James Hutton Brew. Davis played a pivotal role in helping Abina, not only because he seems to have taken her into his care (under conditions about which we know no details), but also because he became her attorney in the courtroom. Much of what is written about Davis in this story is a composite of evidence about other young men like him. As a court interpreter, Davis was likely educated at a mission school whose curriculum would have included English. He also spoke several other languages. He could write, and was likely a Christian. He probably was of mixed heritage, with at least one European ancestor. Although at the bottom of the middle classes

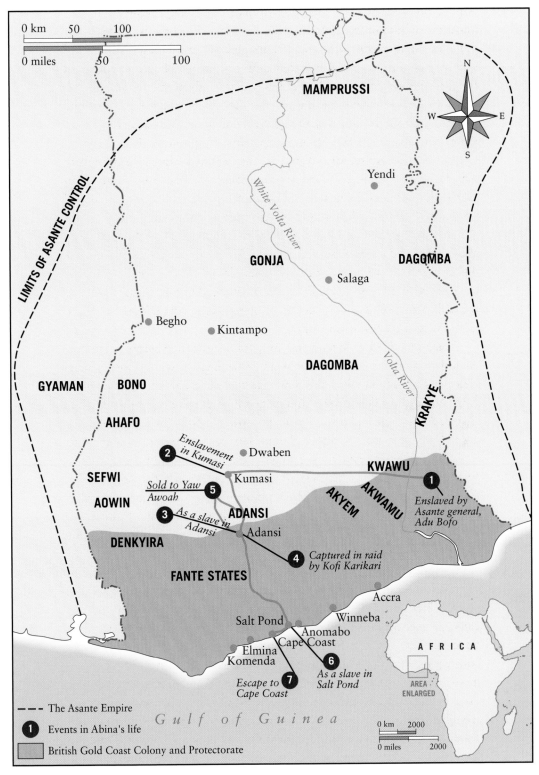

MAP 4 Asante and the Gold Coast, ca. 1876

of Cape Coast, Davis was employed, seems to have been related to an important local merchant family, and understood how to speak the language of the court and appeal to the morality of the judge.

That judge was William Melton, a minor career official of the British Colonial Office. In fact, we don't know that much about Melton, although it's likely that his papers exist somewhere in Britain and that further research in the British archives could tell us more about him. Melton was not trained as a judge, but in his capacity as judge he was reasonably fair, at least as far as cases involving enslavement were concerned. He ruled in favor of plaintiffs who claimed to have been enslaved almost as often as in favor of their alleged masters, and frequently turned to local advisors to help him in his decisions. Unfortunately, those advisors and jurors tended to be powerful men who were sympathetic to slave ownership and not to young, female slaves.

We have constructed our interpretation of Melton's positions in this **graphic history** based partly on the record of his decisions and partly on a profile of other minor officials serving on the Gold Coast during this period. Most were evangelical Christians from the British middle classes who spent only a short time in each of several overseas colonies and who saw themselves as rightfully wielding great power and sacred responsibility toward the African subjects of the British Empire in cases ranging from land ownership disputes to slavery to murder.

Melton seems to have been ambivalent about cases involving alleged slavery, and this ambivalence was especially pronounced in this case because of the presence of James Hutton Brew. We know more about Brew than any other person in this story. The only trained lawyer among the "important men" with whom Abina interacted, Brew was the descendant of an Irish merchant who had married into a powerful local family of chiefs and traders. James Hutton Brew was related to many important local leaders, and he had strong ties to the British authorities. Yet he was also seen by some (although not Melton) as being somewhat suspect. Not only did many British of the time distrust people of mixed heritage, whom they saw as "uppity" or "polluted," but Brew himself had been involved in a scheme called the Fante Confederation in the early 1870s. The goal of this plan was to create an independent local state around Cape Coast. While Brew and his compatriots had hoped to get British support for this state, the administration had in fact seen it as a threat and shut it down quickly, briefly imprisoning Brew and others. Yet this did not mean that Brew was anti-European. In fact, he and the other conspirators had modeled their proposed state on Britain and Germany, and his writings suggest that he truly believed that British "civilization" had much to offer Africans.

Brew was clearly an effective representative for Quamina Eddoo, about whom we know much less. Clearly, Eddoo was a wealthy country "gentleman" who owned many slaves and other dependents, interacted with merchants and traders, and could afford the leading lawyer in the region. Yet he was probably illiterate, and today, nobody who lives in the area of Saltpond, where he lived more than a hundred years ago, appears to know of him. Like Abina, he has virtually disappeared from history as it is written today, and thus he cannot be numbered among the "important men"—Davis, Brew, and Hutton—who dominate the proceedings of the court case that was supposedly between Eddoo and Abina.

PART IV
READING GUIDE

NEA ONN IM NO SUA A, OHU
"HE WHO DOES NOT KNOW CAN KNOW FROM LEARNING"

In Part III of this book, we gave you a sense of the social environment and history surrounding the events portrayed in *Abina and the Important Men*. That background was reconstructed by the author, who put together evidence from primary sources (documents and oral histories collected in the archives and communities of Ghana) and secondary sources (scholarly works by experts on the region's history).

However, historians do more than just reconstruct what they think happened in the past. They also interpret past events. No two authors or two artists would interpret a document like Abina Mansah's testimony in entirely the same ways. Nor should they be expected to do so. Interpreters of the past, like the author and illustrator of this volume, have a public role to play in helping us to make sense of the past in light of our own lives and present experiences. So, instead of just reconstructing the past, we help our readers to construct meaning from those pasts that are relevant today.

Yet, as historians, we do not have total freedom in their interpretations of past events. We also have responsibilities. We have an obligation to the people who lived through those events to talk about their experiences accurately and perhaps empathetically. We also have a duty to our readers to help them to construct their own understandings of the past rather than simply imposing ours upon them. For that reason, Part IV of this book is a guide to the issues of philosophy, ethics, and methods that we faced in turning a document from 1876 into a graphic history in 2011. In the following pages, we grapple with three questions: Whose story is this? Is it a true story? Is it an authentic story? In response to each question, we present a series of related thoughts and issues in increasingly complex levels. The first level of each explanation is meant to be open to all readers. In the second level, we weave in more complex themes and ideas for more advanced readers. Finally, in the third level of each response, we dig deep into the issues, methods, and morals surrounding the interpretation of Abina Mansah's testimony. This section is not the last word on these interpretive themes. In Part V of this volume we revisit Abina's story and our own interpretation in light of the discussions elicited by the first edition of this book, demonstrating that history is produced by historians and communities in a way that is more like an ongoing conversation than a single event.

WHOSE STORY IS THIS?

LEVEL 1: A STAIRCASE OF VOICES

The first question we must ask is, "Whose story is *Abina and the Important Men*?" Like most histories, the story in this volume has multiple characters, all of whom were real people and who have a right to claim some ownership of any account of their lives. There are at least two accounts of the story in question. The first is the transcript on which this book is based. The second is the graphic history itself. Neither the anonymous clerk (possibly Melton himself) who wrote the transcript in 1876, nor the historian who wrote the text of this book, nor the artist who illustrated it were purely objective observers. Rather, each interpreted the events of the story in their own way.

Thus the first answer to this question must be that many people can claim to have participated in the production of this story—Abina and the other actors in the story, the clerk, the historian, the artist, and indeed the readers and scholars who have responded to this book since it was first published. These individuals can be seen to be stairs in a staircase of voices leading from Abina, who brought the case to court and initiated the story, to the reader. Yet from the top stair, it is difficult to see what the stairs beneath look like. In order to get back to the first stair—to Abina—the reader has to be able to move down through the stairs like an archaeologist excavating the distant past by carefully removing and analyzing each layer of soil.

The first layer that must be removed is the one created by the collaborators on this book—the author and the illustrator. As we will discuss in a following section, we have tried to present a reasonably accurate picture of the events described in the transcript. Nevertheless, we know that we have put our own stamp upon the story. The author, especially, approached this story with a particular empathy for Abina. He saw this story as inspirational, for it revealed how a young woman in the lowest rungs of society could still fight for her freedom. He also saw it as a vehicle for explaining the human costs, as well as the historical complexities, of the slave trade, **colonialism**, and the free-market demand for goods like palm oil. The reader may agree that these are admirable goals, but the author still must acknowledge that they reflect today's moral standards in the United States, and may not have been the perspectives of any of the actors in the past. In presenting these themes, the author chose to organize Abina's testimony along the lines of a plot that speaks to him, and to emphasize certain points by putting words in the mouths of Abina, Davis, Melton, and others that they may not have said. The author then produced a script that was interpreted in images by the artist, who depicted some people more sympathetically than others and generally helped to imagine the story along the plot lines proposed by the author.

If we wish to remove the author's and artist's interpretation of events, we can look back to the transcript itself, which is the only direct evidence of events in Abina's life (see Figure 1). However, the transcript is not an exact record of Abina's testimony either. Like most people of her time—and in contrast to Davis, Melton, and Brew—Abina probably could not write. Hence the transcript that is featured in this book was written by an officer of the court. In British courts of law on the Gold Coast, records were usually kept not by the lawyers or the judge, but rather by an official clerk. Yet in *Regina v. Quamina Eddoo* (Abina's case—*Regina* is Latin for "Queen" and refers to Queen Victoria, who was the ruling monarch of Great Britain at that time), the usual clerk of the court seems to have been missing. We know this because this case was recorded in handwriting that differed from most other cases in the same casebook. It's possible that Davis, who was a court interpreter, was also normally the clerk, but that he could not keep the records in this case because he was also serving as legal counsel to Abina.

The switch to a new clerk for the day may have been a fortunate one, for whoever kept the records in Abina's case took unusually extensive notes. The testimony in *Regina v. Quamina Eddoo* is much longer and much more detailed than in comparable cases, thus forming a large enough story for us to work with. It seems likely that Melton himself took the notes, as the handwriting in this case seems to match handwriting in notes Melton wrote elsewhere. But Melton, of course, was not a disinterested observer. He had much at stake in this case—including, perhaps, the political stability of the region and his own career. He probably did not write down the words of Abina or other participants verbatim, as these might not have suited his purpose. And it is likely he could not have even if he wanted to. Most court clerks of the time, whether trained or not, had difficulty following rapid conversation and frequently made errors or omissions. An error can be found, for example, on page 94 of the transcript, where Abina is reported to have said that the other girls were "fed, but not fed." The second "fed" should probably be "paid." Thus in turning the testimony of Abina and others into a court transcript, Melton by mistake or on purpose probably shaped the document and the story it told.

Melton was also a key voice within the transcript in his role as judge, or magistrate. As the final decision maker, he was the one who had to be won over by the participants, and as a result he defined the rules of engagement. Based on the record of his judgments in other cases, we know that Melton seems to have held a somewhat typical British understanding of "slavery." In the first place, he defined enslavement in economic terms and thus looked for proof that the person in question was bought and worked unpaid. Yet he also saw slavery as a breaking of the rules of fatherhood. Adult males, he seems to have believed, had the right to compel children (their own offspring, apprentices, or wards) to work, as well as to punish

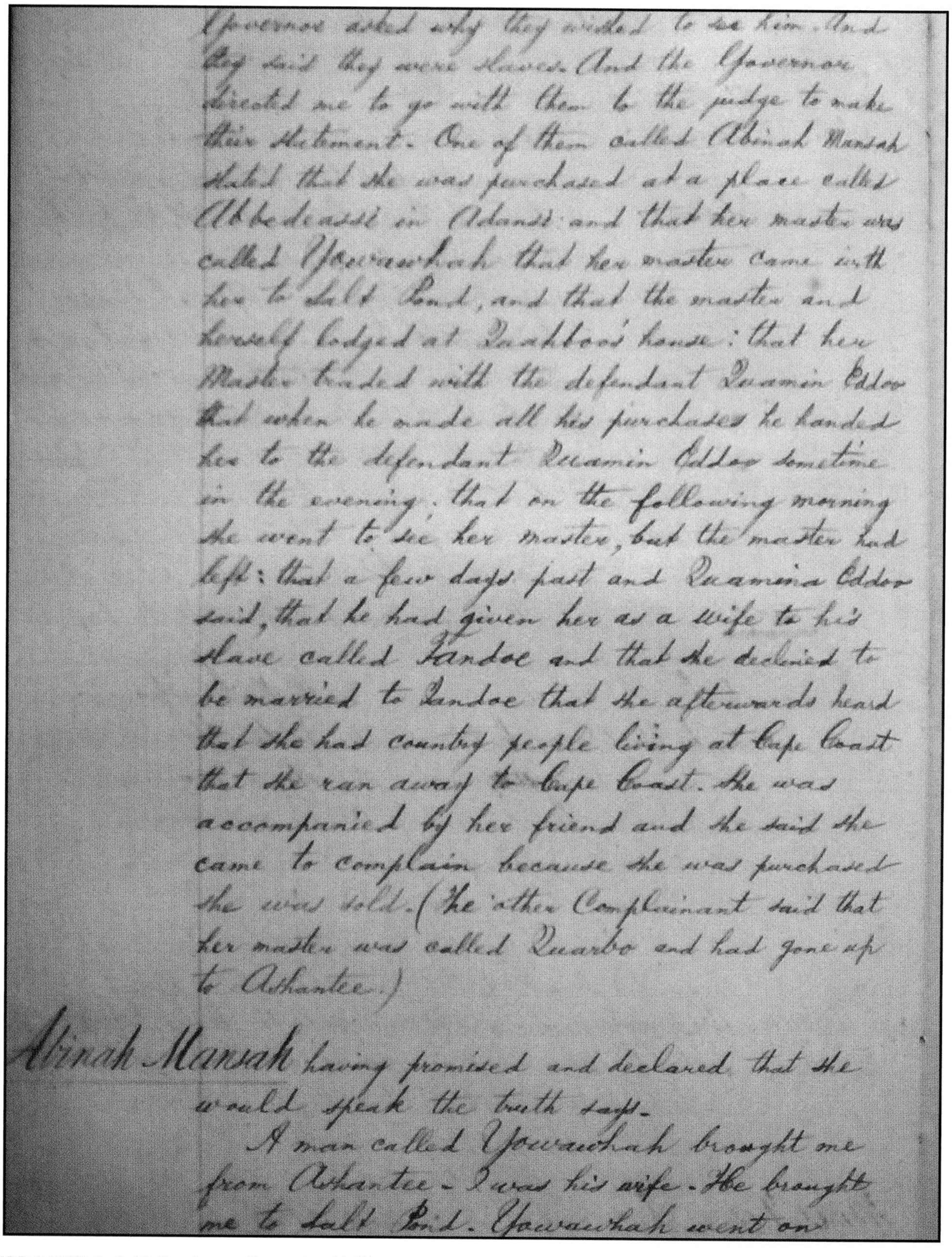
Governor asked why they wished to see him. And
they said they were slaves. And the Governor
directed me to go with them to the judge to make
their statement. One of them called Abinah Mansah
stated that she was purchased at a place called
Abbedeassee in Adansi and that her master was
called Yowawhah that her master came with
her to Salt Pond, and that the master and
herself lodged at Quahboo's house: that her
Master traded with the defendant Quamin Eddoo
that when he made all his purchases he handed
her to the defendant Quamin Eddoo sometime
in the evening. that on the following morning
she went to see her master, but the master had
left: that a few days past and Quamina Eddoo
said, that he had given her as a wife to his
slave called Tandoe and that she declined to
be married to Tandoe that she afterwards heard
that she had country people living at Cape Coast
that she ran away to Cape Coast. She was
accompanied by her friend and she said she
came to complain because she was purchased
she was sold. (The other Complainant said that
her master was called Quarbo and had gone up
to Ashantee.)
Abinah Mansah having promised and declared that she
would speak the truth saith.
A man called Yowawhah brought me
from Ashantee - I was his wife - He brought
me to Salt Pond. Yowawhah went on

FIGURE 1 SCT 5-4-19 *Regina v. Quamina Eddoo*, 10 Nov 1876. This is the file in which Abina's testimony appears. By 1876, British handwriting and notational style had largely been standardized through formal education—men of Melton's class would have been educated in private schools, but Britain also introduced mandatory schooling in 1870. Education largely took the form of rote learning, and penmanship was taught through endless repetition. Readers may note that the scribe (or Melton) spells Abina's name here as "Abinah." British spelling of African names was largely phonetic. For example, Kwame and Kweku were often rendered "Qwame" or "Quecue." Many colonial spellings have been abandoned by Ghanaians, like the "h" at the end of Abina. For specific cases, refer to the note on page xix. Photo by Kojo Bright Botwe, Public Records and Archives Administration Department, Accra, Ghana.

them physically. Slavery, in his view, was evident when this relationship crossed some sort of limits—when the work was inappropriate for the child or when the physical punishment was abusive. This view of adult males as "fathers," with duties to protect and to rule, was common to Britons both at home and abroad in this period. Melton also shared with many other British officials in Africa a need to describe and interpret African rituals and customs, which often influenced his legal judgments. For example, Melton witnessed young Akan husbands-to-be giving ritualistic gifts to their future in-laws and decided that Africans "bought" their wives. And he was clearly very interested in the rituals of "cutting beads" and "giving cloth" mentioned in the trial (and discussed at greater length in Part V). Yet he also filtered local customs through his own lens of nineteenth-century European values, mentioning concepts like "free will," which was then in vogue in British philosophical circles.

James Davis and James Hutton Brew both had some understanding of Melton's legal and philosophical views, and they catered to them during the trial, creating a powerful shared language of "law" and "civilization" that everyone could understand, with the obvious exception of Abina. Oddly, however, Abina's inability to understand may provide an opportunity to excavate her voice from beneath those of the important men. For example, Abina rejects Melton's formulaic interpretation of slavery, and instead tries to speak from the heart about her own experiences. She deflects a complex question by saying simply that "when a free person is sitting down at ease the slave is working," and explains what slavery meant to her: "I had been sold and I had no will of my own and I could not look after my body and health." When asked to comment on whether the other girls in the house might have been slaves—in order to paint her as merely a complainer—she said she could not tell how Eddoo had treated them, "but as for me he did nothing good for me." Some of these quotes may actually be proverbs that were widespread in local society, and may represent a wider "voice" or "truth" than Abina's alone. Nevertheless, it is these moments that help make Abina's story enduring despite the many layers that cover up her voice.

LEVEL 2: SILENCES

While it's possible to look at this story as a staircase of voices *added* on top of one another, it's also important to realize that something was also *lost* at each step of the process. In order to explain this seeming incongruity, we can usefully turn to historian Michel-Rolph Trouillot's argument that history involves the creation of silences as well as voices. In his influential book *Silencing the Past*, Trouillot (who was a professor of anthropology and social sciences at the University of Chicago before his death in 2012) engaged the issue of the ways in which "history" is produced by professional historians.[1] Like many other philosophers of the past few decades, Trouillot argued that historians don't just *reconstruct* the past like detectives searching for clues as to what happened, but they also *construct* the past by putting their own interpretations and spin on their accounts of the past. Moreover, Trouillot argued that because historians' interpretations tend to be accepted, they are particularly powerful in shaping understandings of the past, and also in legitimizing or discounting certain versions of that past. Thus, historians are part of the process by which some voices come to be featured in authoritative accounts of the past and others get left out.

Trouillot specifically suggested that this process of "silencing" some voices has four stages. First, some people's perspectives never get recorded. This is especially true of the illiterate, the poor, women, and in some cases people of color—in short, people like Abina. Second, not all records that are put into archives are saved: Some documents get thrown away; others deteriorate, often because they are considered to have little value. Third, historians choose to feature some sources and voices and to ignore others when they write about the past. Finally, some accounts of the past come to be seen as "classics" or "important," while others are discounted.

Arguably, Abina's voice was silenced in the first stage of the process in that she did not write her own account of what happened. Yet, as we have argued above, by going to court and having her story heard and recorded, Abina made sure that she would not be silenced forever. Without that effort, she—like so many other young, enslaved females—might have disappeared from history forever. As a direct result of her insistence on going to court, and with a little luck, we *can* now hear her. Of course, it is too simple to suggest that the mere finding or even printing of Abina's testimony reverses the silencing. Instead, excavating her voice from within the document requires that we also confront the limitations and processes of representation and translation by which her testimony was turned into a transcript and then a graphic history.

LEVEL 3: REPRESENTATION AND TRANSLATION

This exploration of the issues of representation and translation continue our theme of the relationship between power and knowledge in the writing of history generally and the story of *Abina and the Important Men* specifically. This topic is vital to addressing the questions of accuracy and

---

1   Michel-Rolph Trouillot, *Silencing the Past: Power and the Production of History* (Boston: Beacon Press, 1995).

authenticity in the next sections of this volume. Let's take a moment to examine the graphic history in two ways.

On the one hand, *Abina and the Important Men* is a representation of Abina's story, and not the story itself. The word *representation* here can be taken to mean two things. First, Abina did not present her story firsthand. Instead, while she verbally presented her story in court, it was the clerk, whether Melton or someone else, who *re-presented* it to us in the transcript, in written form. Then the author and artist of this volume represented it once again to the reader. It is vital to understand that no matter how much we (the author and illustrator) or the clerk valued accuracy, we have interfered with the story as Abina first told it.[2]

But there is also a second understanding of *representation*, similar to the way in which a politician represents his or her district, for example. By this definition, the author and illustrator serve as Abina's representatives, since she cannot speak for herself. Are we presenting her experiences and self-image accurately, in a manner that accords with her wishes? We will never be able to fully know. In addition, we must acknowledge that we have more power than Abina in this representation because we have the ability to write, illustrate, and publish her story, something she could never do.[3] Thus we have a particular responsibility to try not to overwrite Abina's story with our own.

On the other hand, what we are doing is making a translation from Abina's world to our own. One of the issues we confronted in writing and illustrating this story accurately was how to interpret Abina's words in the transcript because they sounded strange to our ears. In part, this is because Abina's words were translated from her language (probably Asante Twi, although she seems to have used some words that come from the Ewe language) to English. In part, this challenge has to do with the fact that the English vernacular at the time was different from what it is today. It also probably owes something to Melton's (or the clerk of the day's) rapid and inaccurate transcription. Finally, it is a consequence of the differences between oral and written storytelling, as we are turning spoken word into written text and image, and these two communication methods have different rhythms and styles.

Thus, we continually had to grapple with the issue of how to translate Abina's story from the language and context of the past to our own world. We felt that we had a responsibility not only to keep the story Abina's,

---

2 Edward Said, *Orientalism* (New York: Vintage, 1979), 21.

3 Gayatri Chakravorty Spivak, "Can the Subaltern Speak?," in *Marxism and the Interpretation of Culture*, ed. Cary Nelson and Lawrence Grossberg (Urbana: University of Illinois Press, 1988), 271–313.

but also to produce a volume that was readable and understandable to those who might not want to immerse themselves in years of study of the nineteenth-century Gold Coast. Thus we had to balance the desire to "translate" the story into a modern idiom without sacrificing those qualities that made it Abina's story and not our own. This tension also connects to the issue of "accuracy," which we discuss next.

IS THIS A "TRUE" STORY?

LEVEL 1: RECONSTRUCTING ABINA'S STORY

One of the principal tasks of the historian is to strive to **reconstruct** the past. In other words, historians recognize that events occurred in the past and seek to determine what happened and why. We generally begin this task by conducting *research*. This usually means going to the *archive* or into *the field*. Archives are sites where documents, photographs, and other records from and of the past are stored, organized, and made available for scholarly use. Many of these archives are official: The Library of Congress in Washington, DC, is the most famous archive in the United States, and Abina's case was located in the National Archives of Ghana. However, many archives are unofficial collections of family or organizational papers. Increasingly, archives are digitized and can be found online. *The field* is the term that researchers use when they are collecting nonarchived material, especially oral testimony and archaeological remains.

Of course, the field and the archive are not neutral places. Both are more likely to retain some documents or stories than others. Most archives are full of the writings of "important men," for example, and contain few records of those individuals deemed to be unimportant. Similarly, oral traditions and archaeological remains are not all preserved at the same rate, and many of the stories and perspectives of everyday people get lost over time. In fact, the archive and the field are both places where views of the past are contested every day. Both professional archivists and people on the street rearrange memories and documents, store some with care, and lose others. Sometimes this process is purposeful, and other times merely the result of coincidence or circumstance.

For example, the archives in Ghana once contained many records that over the years have been lost for various reasons. Some were lost temporarily—in fact, the testimony on which this volume was based was misplaced for several years; only their rediscovery by archivists in the last year or two made this second edition possible. Other documents from this era have been permanently lost. Several of the court documents from the period after Abina's case were stored beneath a leaky pipe and have decayed completely. Other documents were written on highly acidic paper, which, combined with the ink that was used, has caused them to slowly deteriorate to the point where they are no longer readable. Still other documents were allegedly sold to private individuals, including tourists, during the 1980s, when archival staff could barely afford to keep up the building in which they were housed.

Because of all these issues, it is impossible for any historian to state truthfully that he or she can tell you "the past as it happened." This is true even when there are many records available, for it would be impossible to record the perspectives of every single person who witnessed an event. Nevertheless, historians generally believe that it is possible to understand certain things about the past, and that there are rules and practices we can follow that increase the likelihood that our reconstructions of the past will yield accurate interpretations.

Accurate reconstructions begin with the historian and his or her attitude toward the evidence. No historian approaches a study of the past completely objectively and dispassionately. For example, the interpretation of *Regina v. Quamina Eddoo*, on which this book is based, is certainly colored by the author's knowledge of the horrors of colonialism and slavery. Nevertheless, it is usually possible to limit the significance of any bias and reach a reasonable conclusion through meticulous research, careful recording, and the placing of all evidence in the correct context.

These practices require the historian to deal with his or her sources extremely carefully. Once, history was largely defined as a craft by the reading of written documents from the past. More recently, historians have learned to work with a variety of sources, including archaeological remains, language, oral traditions, and memories, to name a few. In general, the best practice for investigating the events of the past and determining their causes is to bring together as many of these sources as possible. By doing so, it is possible to create a broad picture of a place and time in the past. These sources can then be read as evidence of what happened to cause a given event, what people were thinking or feeling about the event, and how they experienced it. Each type of source requires a specific set of practices to limit errors in interpretation, and historians are learning more about how to handle these sources all the time.

Of course, the best source in the world is useless if it is poorly misunderstood or if the historian misrecords the evidence. There have been occasions in the past in which historical analyses were incorrect simply because the historian miscopied a statement from a document. In order to avoid those mistakes in this volume, the author had the main original document—the court transcript—carefully photographed. He then copied it onto paper, asking a graduate student to check the copy for errors.

The court transcript by itself is difficult to interpret without a wealth of data that helps us to understand what it means. For example, what is the meaning of the removal of Abina's beads or the giving of cloth? In order to answer these questions, the author discussed these topics with Ghanaians, both professional historians and other inhabitants of the region, and sought out additional documents that might provide answers to these questions. Other important information was contributed by readers and reviewers of the first edition of this volume. Its appearance in this edition helps to make the interpretation more accurate. Even so, the interpretation presented in the graphic novel is not definitive, since it is based on only a few sources. Nevertheless, it does demonstrate the importance of relating a single document to a whole range of sources wherever possible.

The issue of accurately representing the past in this volume was complicated by the illustrator's need to represent Abina's world graphically. A written history of Abina might reasonably omit the question of what Quamina Eddoo's house looked like, or what kind of furniture might have been in Cape Coast Castle, or what clothing Abina likely wore. A graphic history cannot do so, however. The illustrator and author had to find and consult paintings, illustrations, and even photographs from that period to provide the necessary visual information for the reader (see Figure 2).

It is worthwhile to spend a moment considering three specific places in the text where we faced particular issues of accuracy and only partially resolved them. The first has to do with the deposition featured on page 13 of the graphic novel, in which Abina attests to the fact that she was sold by Yaw Awoah, enslaved by Quamina Eddoo, and told to marry Tandoe or else suffer a flogging. In fact, the deposition has been lost. We infer its presence by a question, early in the trial, that Davis posed to Abina: "What is read to you now did you not make that statement?" The contents of the statement are unclear, although from the topics leading up to Davis's question and based on his knowledge of the law at the time, it probably included the fact that Abina Mansah had been brought into the Protectorate illegally, had been sold, and had been threatened with physical punishment. However, we cannot be sure.

In fact, Abina's relationships and interactions with Davis are difficult to characterize. On the one hand, in his statement to Melton that opens the court transcripts, Davis alleges that Abina and another woman merely approached him and begged him to intercede on their behalf. However, it would have been highly unusual for even an ambitious court interpreter like Davis to have petitioned a court on the behalf of a woman entirely unknown to him. Moreover, there are other recorded cases in which constables and clerks went to court on behalf of women or children whom they

HAULING SIR GARNET WOLSELEY UP TO GOVERNMENT HOUSE

RETURNED FROM THE ASHANTEE WAR   SIR GARNET WOLSELEY'S RECEPTION BY THE NATIVE LADIES

FIGURE 2 "The Ashantee War—Return of Sir Garnet Wolseley to Cape Coast Town," *Graphic* (London), April 11, 1874, p. 330. Images such as this were invaluable in providing information about the time and place and the people who inhabited it. Illustrator Liz Clarke looked at many pictures of both historical and contemporary Ghana to better understand its visual identity. This image specifically offered details about the style of clothing and architecture of the time. The exterior of Davis's house is modeled on the one at bottom right. © The British Library Board. (HS.74/1099)

claimed had approached them unsolicited, only to learn through the testimony that they actually had longstanding relationships (sexual, familial, or labor) with these individuals. For that reason, the interpretation in this volume speculates a longer relationship existed between Abina and Davis.

The second episode that needs some elaboration has to do with the jury discussion. We in fact know nothing about this jury specifically or what they deliberated. We know who was likely to have been asked to sit on a jury during this period, based on other cases in which the names of the jurors are actually listed. Those jurors we can identify were all men, and usually either chiefly officeholders or leading "educated men"—English-speaking professionals like Brew. We have some idea as to the arguments such men had presented in 1874 to try to stop emancipation (see Part III), and we demonstrate those on pages 72–73. In general, these arguments posit either that slavery in the Gold Coast was customary and rather benign, with the master as a father figure protecting young people rather than exploiting them, or that disrupting the slave-labor economy would slow down the region's economic development. Slave owners had learned that these were the arguments most accepted by British magistrates and officials. We do not know that any of the jurors said these things during the deliberations in Abina's case, but it seems likely.

As these examples illustrate, it is impossible to know the "whole truth" about any event, especially one with as few direct sources as this court case. In order to tell the story, therefore, we have had to employ techniques such as referring to similar sources and deducing the contents of documents from references in other sources. These are not exact practices, but without them it would be impossible to construct even an approximate interpretation of Abina's experiences.

LEVEL 2: DECONSTRUCTING THE COURTROOM TRANSCRIPT

Of course, historians don't just reconstruct the past from documents. They also **deconstruct** narratives of the past. Deconstruction is a term that often sounds like some sort of trendy, high-theory concept of little practical use. In fact, however, deconstruction is a way of getting at *truths* beyond the obvious, and is therefore highly useful in expanding the range of information we can extract out of documents, images, and other sources from the past.

Most sources contain intentional messages—that is, they were produced by some person or persons for the purpose of conveying information to an audience. Oral, written, and visual sources can all contain intentional messages. Whether a document like the U.S. Constitution, a folk story like "Little Red Riding Hood," or a painting like the ceiling of the Sistine Chapel, all were meant to communicate meaning to an audience. Often, the meaning is open to debate, as is evidenced by the ongoing dispute of the intentions of the framers of the U.S. Constitution that still shapes politics in the United States today. Nevertheless, it is clear that there *are* intentional messages in this document. We call the practice of seeking to understand the information or messages that the authors of the text wanted to convey to their audience **reading with the grain**. Reading with the grain is an important skill to develop, as it requires the researcher to try to understand the writers' ideas and purpose and to see the world from his or her perspective.

However, texts also contain messages that their authors did not intend to convey to their audience. Often these messages are sets of assumptions. For example, when Abina testified to the giving of cloth or the breaking of her beads, she assumed her audience would know what that meant—that it signified a transfer in her "belonging," either within a family group or to a master. She did not feel the need to explain the meaning of these messages. Of course, Melton had no idea that these acts were metaphors for belonging, because he did not speak the same language and operate with the same set of assumptions as Abina. So, too, the historian today might easily gloss over these events described by Abina, seeing them as acts of violence but nothing more, if he or she merely read the court transcript with the grain.

It is necessary, therefore, to **read against the grain**—or to deconstruct our sources—in order to gain access to the assumptions. The practice of deconstruction generally involves a series of steps. The first of these is to establish the origins, author, and other evidentiary issues about the text and to read it with the grain. It is especially important to know as much as possible about the author—his or her status in society, life experiences, political and cultural outlook, and so forth. This is because the assumptions we are looking for are usually generated communally and shared among a group. In the case of the "important men" in this story, for example, a British version of paternalism (the legitimate role of the father or other adult male figure as protector and punisher) seems to have been shared because of the shared life experiences of Davis, Melton, and Brew. Abina, however, did not have the same set of assumptions.

The next step in deconstruction requires the researcher to search for assumptions and figurative language—metaphors, similes, stereotypes, and the like. Often, it is useful to look at a range of documents as a way of identifying language that is commonly used by many people in the same society or social group. At the same time, it is important to read the document closely to see where explanations end and assumptions begin—in other words, to search out the points that the author assumes need no explanation. The famous anthropologist Clifford Geertz (1926–2006) explains this problem by using the example of winks, and points out the difficulty of an outsider understanding the meaning of a wink as a gesture.

Only by investigating the many roles of the wink in a society—lascivious, indicating agreement, mocking—and by understanding the exact situation in which a particular wink takes place can the outsider hope to understand what the wink actually means.[4]

The transcript of Abina's testimony was recorded purposefully but not necessarily with the intent that it be read in the future, let alone turned into a graphic history. It therefore contains several intentional messages, meant to influence the courtroom proceedings, and a number of inadvertent meanings. Through deconstruction, it is possible to identify two very different sets of assumptions that were operating in the courtroom, and thus two very different versions of "truth."

The first—and dominant—set of assumptions evident in the transcript is a construction of the world that defined Melton, shared to a certain extent by Brew, and aspired to by Davis. This view might be called "Whiggish," after the slang term **"Whig,"** for the liberal, middle-class political alignment of the time. In this view, progress is possible along rational terms. Good order is represented by rational people—especially adult men—acting on behalf of those assumed to be less rational than they, especially children, the disabled, and women. By 1876, many middle-class Britons adopted a view in which Africans and other non-Europeans (and the Irish and eastern and southern Europeans as well) were seen as being less rational than the Britons and other northern Europeans. This racialized view of peoples from different social and cultural backgrounds still persists in Europe and the United States today. However, *race* was largely defined at this time through the idea of *rationality*, and men such as Brew and Davis seem to have interpreted being *civilized* in an English sense, in which civilized individuals can make rational decisions.

For Britons and others in the late nineteenth century who espoused this view, slavery was generally seen as a negative institution—something of a reversal from earlier decades—in that it held back progress and conflicted with "free labor," "the free market," and other desirable economic institutions. Moreover, slavery represented the opposite of rationality since it was irrational and restricted the liberal, capitalist system of labor and society. Indeed, the word *free* is perhaps the hallmark of the Whiggish perspective. This is expressed in the transcript not only by Melton's understanding of slavery as the opposite of freedom, but also by his interesting question, early in Abina's testimony, of whether she had "free will." *Free will* was a term that had been in

---

4   Clifford Geertz, *The Interpretation of Cultures* (New York: Basic Books, 1977), 6–7. Geertz is himself building on the work of philosopher Gilbert Ryle.

vogue in Britain, and was discussed by many of the leading bourgeois British intellectuals, including John Locke (1632–1704), David Hume (1711–1776), and John Stuart Mill (1806–1873). Indeed, Mill at least had queried whether non-Europeans could be said to have free will at all. By asking about this concept, Melton appears to have been getting at the heart of the "truth" of the matter, as far as the Whiggish view of slavery was concerned—was Abina free, or was she constrained, restrained, and captive? By reading the document against the grain, we can see Melton's assumptions, and those he shared with Davis and Brew, about how the world worked.

The specific philosophical concept of free will, however, had little meaning to Abina because Abina operated outside of the Whiggish assumptions of the way the world did and should work. In fact, she did not come to court to achieve her freedom. She had already done so by successfully fleeing to Cape Coast. Nor does she seem to have been in much danger of being recaptured. There are few records of slave owners from the countryside successfully reclaiming their former captives in Cape Coast, and it's not likely that this was a great risk. We can instead believe that Abina had come to court to tell a different "truth."

Abina's truth emerges from closely reading some of her statements, several of which are featured as full pages in the graphic history. First, reading with the grain, we can see that Abina tries to convey her enslavement to Melton and the men of the courtroom, not in some abstract sense of not being *free* but as something experienced bodily and psychologically. Thus she complains that she "could not look after [her] body and health." She rejects Brew's questions about the status of the other girls in the house by saying she knew little of their long-term experiences: "But *as for me* he did nothing good for me . . . and I ran away." The episodes on which she chooses to focus are also both physically and psychologically affecting— the violent cutting of the beads, the threat of flogging, the forced engagement to Tandoe. These episodes, and their lingering effects, are part of Abina's "truth."

This brings us to the question of why Abina chose to litigate against her former owner in the first place. Assuming she was facing little threat of re-enslavement (a possibility she does not even mention), she must have had a deeper purpose for bringing him to court. One of our interpretations is that Abina's testimony is a plea to be heard, a willingness to bear witness against injustice, and an attempt to deal with the pain of surviving such a violent system. Another part of our interpretation, having to do with her specific experiences as a woman, is discussed in Part V. Both interpretations reflect the strength of a remarkable individual and the suffering of a whole class of people over time.

LEVEL 3: RECONSTRUCTING ABINA'S "TRUTHS" OR CONSTRUCTING OUR OWN?

Yet does the above conclusion really reflect Abina's message, or have we imposed on this story a message based on our values, stories, and moral codes? Is this truly what Abina was thinking, or have we created a heroine who suits our own needs? In other words, have we really reconstructed Abina's "truth" by deconstructing her message, or have we constructed a story that reflects our truths today?

Some scholars argue that reconstructing the past is impossible, and that both the tasks of reconstruction and deconstruction lead us only to create versions of the past that are meaningful to us but would be unrecognizable to people living in the past. They argue, in fact, that historians really only **construct** pasts. In the extreme, proponents of this argument suggest that there is no such thing as *truth*, only interpretations, or, as the French theorist Jacques Derrida (1930–2004) wrote, perhaps "there is nothing outside of the text."[5] In this theory, all language and writing, including history, is merely a representation of the world that is meaningful to the writer.

Such a view is of limited use to the historian. To be sure, it is important that historians recognize the difference between *events* that happened in the past and *interpretations* of those events. There is general agreement among the current generation of historians, for example, that history can be neither truly objective nor entirely authoritative. Nevertheless, most historians (if not scholars in all other fields) agree that it is possible to strive to capture some message, metaphor, or "truth" about the past.

Of more immediate importance to us here is the work of historian and literary critic Hayden White (currently a professor emeritus at the University of California, Santa Cruz). Building on the idea that historians, like other humans, are caught in webs of meaning and not entirely free to interpret the past outside of their own social situation, White suggests that we interpret history through a limited set of ideologies available to us, and thus have only a few plots into which we try to fit past narratives and events. He focuses especially on historians trained in the period since the emergence of professional history in the late nineteenth century, and argues that all histories in the Western tradition since then are written from anarchist, conservative, radical, or liberal ideologies. He then connects these ideologies to just four plots. One of these is what White calls the "romantic" plot, which embodies certain values in an individual and then celebrates their victory over a series of challenges and obstacles. In particular, these values are the values of the author and some segment of

---

5 Jacques Derrida, *Of Grammatology* (Baltimore: Johns Hopkins University Press, 1998). Originally printed 1976.

his or her society.[6] So, for example, it's possible to argue that the interpretation of Abina's story in this book tells us more about the author's and illustrator's values of *freedom*, multicultural diversity, and gender equity than anything about nineteenth-century West Africa.

This is perhaps accurate. However, anthropologist Jan Vansina (currently a professor emeritus of anthropology and history at the University of Wisconsin, Madison) and historian Carolyn Hamilton (professor of social anthropology at the University of Cape Town, South Africa) have both pointed to the fact that stories aren't just made up out of nowhere. There are continuities to interpretations over time and across multiple narrators and authors. In fact, some voices in the historical record seem to yell out and to say exactly what they mean, with relatively little room for free interpretation. Abina's voice is one of these. In the courtroom, she is forceful enough to receive unquestionably the most extensive treatment given by any testifying female former slave in a Gold Coast colonial court. Her words are powerful enough to form a consistent message that is a desire to be heard as well as to be free. It is for this reason, and through our attempts to provide broad contextualization and careful qualification of our work, that we are confident enough to say that her message is present in our interpretation.

IS THIS "AUTHENTIC" HISTORY?

LEVEL 1: LOCAL FORMS OF HISTORY-TELLING

There is something special about a story of a family's past told by a grandmother or grandfather in the kitchen on a special family day. When these histories are told to us, we rarely question whether they are exactly *accurate* or what *message* they convey. Their value lies somewhere else, in the sense of community they create and the continuity of existence they reinforce. This value can be expressed by their *authenticity*. The concept of authenticity suggests that the rituals and ways we pass on information about the past are part of a wider sense of who we are as families, communities, and nations.

There is a catch, however. Neither a scholarly article nor a textbook nor even a graphic history fits within the way that most people in Cape Coast and its surrounding regions talk about who they are. Perhaps it is appropriate to illustrate this point with an argument. Several years ago, I (Trevor) was conducting interviews around Cape Coast to find out what

---

6 Hayden White, *Metahistory: The Historical Imagination in Nineteenth-Century Europe* (Baltimore: Johns Hopkins University Press, 1973).

people knew about an event that had happened during roughly 1867 to 1873, ending barely three years before Abina's court case. Called the **Fante Confederation**, it was quite a famous event, often cited in African history textbooks and Ghanaian official histories. Moreover, the Akan speakers of the Cape Coast region tend to very effectively pass on oral histories of important events. Therefore, I had reasonable expectations of learning something. Yet time and again, the everyday people of the region reported that they knew nothing of it. I finally found some individuals who *were* able to tell me what they knew about the events. Yet their stories were all oddly familiar, and it turned out that they were merely repeating the lessons they learned from their high school textbooks. So here we had a story that scholars and the government claimed had "historical importance" to the region, and yet it was not reproduced in the popular ways of talking about the past.

There are several popular modes in the coastal region of Ghana by which the past is discussed today. These range from rumors and family stories passed along informally from generation to generation, to proverbs, to epic foundation myths and historical narratives of central social importance ritually related to the public, or in secret ceremonies by members of *asafo* companies. Perhaps the most widely recognized of these processes of transmission, however, is through the state linguist of each of the small *aman* (plural of oman), or "traditional areas" of the country. These state linguists have the Akan name *okyeame*, and they are individuals whose job it is to recall past events and parables for the use of the community and its rulers.

Most aman have several linguists, each representing an *abusua* (matrilineal group) within the community. One of these individuals is usually considered the *chief linguist* and represents the entire state. Part of the linguists' job is to commune with the ancestors, a role that carries a great deal of responsibility for relating stories about the past as advice for contemporary rulers and members of society. In some situations, linguists act as private advisors; in others, their role is very public—for example, in the rituals that define the calendar, the stages of life, and the public identity of the community. Often, they are called upon to speak at these events, both in prayer and in story.

The historical narratives related by the okyeame bear only a limited relationship to those of the history textbooks of Western societies. For one thing, they are only rarely chronological, instead jumping backward and forward in time to make important points. They are rarely written, but rather spoken and sung, sometimes both together. Often, they take the shape of performances, and even include props. Both the singing and the props are meant to help aid the memory of the linguist in order to maintain accuracy, but the spoken sections are there to purposefully allow the linguist to adapt the story to the situation in which it is being told. Thus a certain amount of improvisation is prized, unlike in our formal histories. On the other hand, like many of our own histories, their stories contain lessons or morals, are represented as having some sort of "truths," and are believed to be of educational value, especially for training the young and new members of society.

In *Abina and the Important Men*, we are moving away from the formal history textbook model, but we are certainly not claiming to have effectively reproduced the narrative styles or skills of the okyeame. A graphic history is a type of history all its own and different from both a traditional history text or the narrative of an okyeame. However, in our use of flashbacks and our attempt to combine writing and graphics, we have tried to gain access to a cadence and techniques that would be familiar to many southern Ghanaians today. We have done this partly in recognition of our duty to produce a history of Ghanaians that would be recognizable and useful *by* Ghanaians today. Indeed, it is our plan that this book will be made available in Ghana to a Ghanaian audience.

LEVEL 2: THE PERSONAL AND THE COLLECTIVE AUTHENTIC

Another level of authenticity has us asking whether Abina would recognize herself in this story. Of course, this question links up with many of the methodological and philosophical issues raised in earlier sections. It also connects to two of the main approaches to the study of the past in the discipline today—**social history** and **cultural history**.

Social history, which emerged out of the political and social developments of the 1960s, developed as a method to understand the experience of large groups of people, largely through the categories of race, class, and gender. It successfully shifted the focus away from the histories of a few elite men (and women), and by looking at everyday behaviors—consumption, entertainment, work, childrearing, sexuality—it came much closer than earlier elite, political models of history to describing an experience that would have been recognizable to most members of a society.

By the 1970s and 1980s, however, some historians identified certain limitations to social history. Specifically, while describing the experiences and behaviors of large groups of people, social historians were less successful in looking at individual variations in both experience and perspective. Influenced by innovations in the field of anthropology, these historians began to focus on "culture" as a central theme. Scholars like Peter Burke (emeritus professor of cultural history at the University of Cambridge) and Lynne Hunt (currently a professor of history at the University of California, Los Angeles) focused less on the shared experiences of categories or groups of people and more on the ways in which individuals related to these collective institutions and behaviors. In doing so, they brought to the fore the idea of *culture*. Cultural historians largely see culture as a web of ideas, meaning, and expressions. Individuals, they argue, get caught up in these webs and are not entirely free to act exactly as they want. However, they also relate to these webs in particular ways and from unique perspectives, and thus make very personal choices. For cultural historians, it is not possible to reduce the individual to a face in the crowd. Just as social historians had sought to write new histories in which groups other than elites could recognize themselves, cultural historians constructed pasts in which individuals might recognize themselves. Yet cultural history also has limitations. One of these is that by seeking individual experiences, cultural historians often end up focusing on the fringes, and not adequately describing the experiences of most people.[7]

Of course, it is possible to make the argument that both of these approaches aim at greater accuracy, rather than some distinct type of authenticity. But this would ignore the motivations that drove both social and later cultural historians. Social historians have frequently focused on class, race, and gender from Marxian, feminist, antiracialist, and other such political positions. They seek to understand the operations of power by elites upon less powerful groups of people and to chronicle and/or commemorate the everyday experiences or grassroots rebellions of these groups. Similarly, cultural historians' decisions to focus on the fringes are often exacerbated by their desire to highlight the oppression suffered by individuals who are seen as being outside of the norm. It is often this aim that drives their emphasis on human variation.

In writing *Abina*, we are seeking a certain authenticity in the model of both a social and a cultural history. On the one hand, we are using Abina as a vehicle for describing the behaviors and experiences of a large group of people—enslaved girls in late nineteenth-century Gold Coast. There are statistical data to show that this group existed in substantial numbers, and court records are the main sources for us to understand their lives. The data from these court records, developed through social history methodologies, illustrate many of the things experienced by Abina—for example, violence, employment, living conditions, and sexual exploitation. Moreover, we sympathize with members of this exploited class and argue that it is of value to know about their experiences.

At the same time, *Abina and the Important Men* is very much a cultural history. First, Abina cannot be assumed to be just like every other

---

7   Paula Fass, "Cultural History/Social History: Some Reflections on a Continuing Dialogue," *Journal of Social History*, 37 (2003), 39–46.

enslaved, young female African living in the Gold Coast in 1876. Indeed, she was probably quite exceptional. Thus, we are using her words to try to understand her individual experiences and personal purposes that drive her actions. In doing so, we are also sympathizing with Abina specifically, and committing ourselves to try to understand the case through *her* eyes.

LEVEL 3: HISTORY AS A FORUM OR A TEMPLE

The search for authenticity has certain limitations, and indeed potential dangers. Most important, it can turn history into **heritage**. There is a difference between the two ways of accessing the past. For all of its problems, *history* at least aspires to critically question the narratives of the past and provide evidence about them. By contrast, *heritage* is an uncritical celebration of history, an attempt to build up in-group identification. This often takes the guise of attacks on other groups. *Authenticity* in the guise of heritage can often be highly orthodox, leading to attacks on those deemed *unauthentic* or different. Moreover, because the search for authenticity doesn't always prize accuracy, it can frequently lead us away from learning as much as we possibly can.

The important point here is that the question of how to interpret the events and experiences of the past is constantly contested among various groups, each with a stake in portraying its events and experiences in particular ways. These contests aren't problems in and of themselves: Such debates are one way that human societies work out their identities; and this is the way the world works, after all. Sometimes contests over the past contribute to hatred or violence, but most often history is used simply to cover up or justify the real issues beneath conflicts. However, the question remains as to how we as historians should react to these contests. Should we pick a side and jump in? Or should we rather strive to be objective and sit above the debate? This is a problem that is at the heart of the public role of the historian.

One useful way into this question comes from the part of our profession that deals with museums. Museums that deal with history, of course, also deal with heritage. Once, museums would have claimed to represent neutral exhibits, in which the facts spoke for themselves. In reality, however, there is no such thing as a truly neutral museum or exhibit. Just as with scholarly books, "facts" and objects in a museum are always presented in such a way and accompanied by such devices as written or audio captions and catalogs as to tell a story that has a particular plot or point of view determined by the curators. Most such exhibits are meant to somehow reinforce the "authentic" heritage story of a group—the "nation of immigrants" story at Ellis Island, for example, or the "brave Texans" story at the Alamo. By contrast, evidence that contradicts this narrative is ignored or hidden.[8] In such cases, the museum becomes a "temple" where people of a particular group can celebrate or commemorate their "authentic" story of their past.

The problems with this type of presentation came to the fore in the United States in a debate in the early 1990s concerning an exhibit dealing with the dropping of two nuclear bombs on Japan. The exhibit was being planned for the Smithsonian Air and Space Museum in Washington, DC, and the museum's director wanted to avoid making the exhibit into a heritage temple. Instead, he wanted it to become a forum in which opposing views on the dropping of the two bombs could be presented and visitors to the museum could be asked to reflect critically on the events. This proposal drew the ire of several groups of "patriots," and especially groups representing military veterans, who felt that such an approach sullied the contributions of those in the military to the winning of the war. They pushed for an approach that would celebrate military service.[9] By contrast, a large group of professional historians campaigned to maintain the forum function of the exhibit by including multiple viewpoints.

A somewhat similar debate has taken place over the years at Cape Coast Castle, the site where Abina's case against Quamina Eddoo was heard. The museum is now a United Nations (UNESCO) World Heritage site and houses a museum. There has been a great deal of debate about the form and content of that museum. As a major site at which Africans were sold to European and American slave ship captains, the castle is a site of pilgrimage and heritage for many African-Americans and Africans of the diaspora. The main story they want to see represented at the museum, of course, has to do with Cape Coast Castle's role as a slave-trading station. Many of these heritage visitors also want to make sure the castle remains unrestored and in dilapidated condition appropriate to a story of suffering and persecution. This means that the room where Abina's case was probably held, for example, remains unfurnished and unrestored. By contrast, many Ghanaians today see Cape Coast Castle as a symbol of colonial persecution rather than of the slave trade. Some Ghanaians believe the museum should be restored to the furniture and condition of the

---

8   Richard R. Flores, "The Alamo: Myth, Public History, and the Politics of Inclusion," in *Contested Histories in Public Space: Memory, Race, and Nation*, ed. Daniel J. Walkowitz and Lisa Maya Knauer (Durham, NC: Duke University Press, 2009), 123–135.

9   Edward T. Linenthal, "Anatomy of a Controversy," in *History Wars: The Enola Gay and Other Battles for America's Past*, ed. Edward Linenthal and Tom Englehardt (New York: Metropolitan, 1996), 9–62.

colonial period, to better illustrate how the colonizers lived and governed the region. Finally, the staff members of the museum wish to present a national story in the museum covering the long history of the castle and local community, rather than focusing solely on the slave trade era.[10] Central to this debate is the question of the role of Africans in the Atlantic slave trade at this museum. Some tour guide operators in the area, for example, would prefer not to acknowledge that Africans were active participants in selling other Africans because this conflicts with a story of African/African-American unity that is at the core of the way that they present a heritage story of the region to visitors. Most of the museum staff, however, is trained to present the *empirical truth*—that is, that there *is* evidence of Africans participating in the slave trade, if not in the same ways as Europeans. To their credit, some official museum guides have even learned how to make a *forum* of the issue, presenting multiple sides of the scholarly and popular debate over the topic.

Abina and the Important Men is intended to be a similar forum on the past, if in a printed, graphic form. To be sure, as author and illustrator we speak with the authority of the historian and get to tell the main narrative of the story in a way that we like. However, we acknowledge that there are many issues within that need a more complex resolution than a single story can provide. How should we view Melton and British claims to "civilization," for example? Should we give Britain credit for legally abolishing slavery in its holding on the Gold Coast, or point out the limitations and hypocrisies of their policies? How should we view Quamina Eddoo and other Africans who, by the nineteenth century, profited from the labor of young Africans themselves? What about Brew, a onetime leader of a local nationalist movement, at once believing in self-rule and self-worth of Africans and yet aspiring to European values and styles of living, and speaking of moral values while defending a slave owner?

It would be all too easy to make a story of Abina and her encounter with a group of powerful men into a temple to her and to the practices and authority of professional historians. We have chosen to avoid that route, and to reveal to you the limitations of our work and the complexities of the story instead. Thus we offer *Abina and the Important Men* to you as a forum, for better or for worse. If we are authentic to no particular view of the past, we hope that we have given the reader something to think about.

---

10   Edward M. Bruner, "Tourism in Ghana: The Representation of Slavery and the Return of the Black Diaspora," *American Anthropologist*, 98 (1996), 290–304.

PART V
ENGAGING *ABINA*

NEA NYANSAPO
"WISDOM KNOT"

long before a discussion with Sue Gonzalez, a U.S.-based teacher who spends her summers teaching literacy classes in Ghana. In the summer of 2013, Sue brought *Abina and the Important Men* with her as a classroom resource. She reported to me that some of the girls she taught—who were decidedly *not* slaves—nevertheless recognized many elements of Abina's story in their own lives. This feedback made us recognize that this volume needed a deeper consideration of the meaning of "slave" in the context of Abina's life experiences. Moreover, the complexity of these issues led us to recruit some leading scholars to help give the question the complex consideration it deserves.

As you read the two sections below, we urge you to think about more than just the content in each section. Rather, consider the ways in which the discussions and feedback that followed the publication of the first edition of *Abina and the Important Men* provided value to this study, and the wider implications of this revision process for history as a collaborative act.

GENDERING *ABINA*

In Laura Mitchell's contribution to the 2012 H-World discussion of the first edition of this book, she noted the following:

> Though the book focuses on the relationship between a slave woman, men with access to varying degrees of power, and the colonial state, its treatment of gender is superficial, and does not appear to engage with the rich corpus of available work on gender in African history. Abina's sexuality and sexual availability, her connections to powerful men, the ability of men to transfer her body and labor, social expectations of marriage and/or sexual relationships based on rank or class aren't directly addressed.[2]

Mitchell's criticism was a challenge to further **gender** Abina's story. Note that *gender* here is being used as a verb, rather than a noun. This choice of syntax signals a significant shift in historical studies. When scholars use *gender* as a noun, we suggest we are going to study sexuality, the division of labor between men and women, love and marriage, and other related topics as part of a particular set of subjects. These subjects are thus set apart from other topics like commerce, governance, or food production. When scholars use *gender* as a verb, however, it implies an understanding

---

2   Laura Mitchell, "Abina Forum," H-World, March 23, 2012, 20:28:36.

of gender as existing everywhere and as part of everything. Gender infuses politics, economics, culture, individual and group identity, and social organization. To gender a study, therefore, means to examine a topic in a place and time through the lens of gender.

The importance of this approach was made clear by the American historian Joan Scott in her highly significant and much cited 1986 article "Gender: A Useful Category of Historical Analysis."[3] In this article, Scott brought together a few important arguments being made by scholars in different fields. Her foundational argument was that gender is at least partly constructed, rather than intrinsic. In other words, when we talk about gender we aren't talking so much about actual, physical differences but rather about the ways that societies understand and represent men, women, and other gendered categories. This finding was enriched by the work of pioneering West African scholars Ifi Amadiume and Oyeronke Oyewumi, whose contemporaneous work showed that different societies may have very distinct assumptions and ideas about gender. Oyewumi contended, for example, that there was no single category of "woman" in Yoruba society, but rather separate categories such as wife, mother, sacred interpreter, and elder, all of which were normally occupied by females.[4] Amadiume, working some years earlier, had similarly argued that women in the Igbo-speaking community she studied were in some circumstances accorded forms of male status.[5]

Scott and the scholars who followed her also argued that social representations of gender are not passive, but rather are fought over and contested in a host of social settings, symbols, relationships, and operations that happen in daily life. Even communications and experiences that are not necessarily *about* gender on the surface often contain implicit conceptions of gender. It follows that if we study the way that gender plays a role in the events and experiences described in any place or time, regardless of the topic, we can stand to gain increased understanding. Using these insights, African historians have recently shown the way that African societies create representations of gender and how gendered experiences shape politics, economics, and social organization in Africa. For example, Emily Lynn Osborn recently demonstrated how different ideas about the household, and the roles of men and women within them, underwrote political

3   Joan Scott, "Gender: A Useful Category of Historical Analysis," *American Historical Review*, 91 (1986), 1053–1075.

4   Oyeronke Oyewumi, *The Invention of Women: Making an African Sense of Western Gender Discourses* (Minneapolis: University of Minnesota Press, 1997).

5   Ifi Amadiume, *Male Daughters, Female Husbands: Gender and Sex in an African Society* (London: Zed Books, 1987).

power in the precolonial West African state of Baté.[6] She shows readers that ideas and practices of marriage, adoption, and motherhood were linked to the way that religious and political leaders could exert power, and convincingly argues that studying state governance outside of these ideas and practices had led earlier scholars to misunderstand what was going on in Baté.

Gendered theories and approaches to historical studies have implications for our reading of Abina's narrative, as well, because gender plays a deep role in at least three aspects of her story. First, gender was related to the condition of enslavement in the Gold Coast during the period of early colonialism. Second, gender was present in the colonial courtroom through British attitudes of paternalism. Third, gender was at the heart of Abina's motives in bringing her case to court, as she sought to navigate a route from shame to respectability through the institution of marriage. This last point is perhaps the most important result of the gendering of Abina's story—so much so that it may fundamentally shift our interpretation of her actions.

GENDER AND SLAVERY IN THE GOLD COAST

The first step in gendering Abina's story is to explore the close connection between gender and enslavement—and especially between being a woman and being a slave—in the nineteenth-century Gold Coast. Evidence from the era suggests that slaves in this place and time—especially around Cape Coast—were overwhelmingly female. There may have been a number of reasons for this connection, but probably the most significant have to do with labor, sex, and reproduction.

In the first place, the Gold Coast was a region with a historic labor shortage. Population densities were quite low before the twentieth century, and the many local resources and products drove a demand for workers. The clearing of forests for fields was worker-intensive, and this coupled with the high demand for laborers to mine gold and harvest kola nuts may have held been one reason that Atlantic slave traders were not able to purchase captives here in the sixteenth and early seventeenth centuries. Once the region was drawn into this trade by rising prices for slaves—after about 1670—it seems that European and American merchants largely wanted to purchase male captives, believing they would work harder than women. As a result, enslaved females may have become concentrated in the coastal region, while male captives were sold into the Atlantic trade at higher rates. This differential was probably exacerbated by the fact that Akan-speaking

6   Emily Osborn, *Our New Husbands are Here: Households, Gender and Politics in a West African State from the Slave Trade to Colonial Rule*, (Athens: Ohio University Press, 2011).

men (unlike European slave traders) may have preferred to retain female captives coming to the coast as laborers in their own homes and farms.

The preference for women probably expanded as palm oil production increased, for the processing of palm oil was widely seen as a woman's task. Some of this processing could be done by a man's wife or wives, for it was generally recognized that men owned their wives' labor (but not their personhood). However, as plantations grew in size, more labor was needed. Thus retaining women in the coastal region allowed entrepreneurial men to increase their production of palm oil, the primary good that could be exchanged for cash and further increase men's wealth.[7]

Owning female captives or slaves also increased a man's ability to produce more offspring and his access to sex. This is a topic that isn't as unrelated to labor as it might seem, because one way for important men to increase their labor pool was by having more children. However, in matrilineal Akan society, children were generally regarded as belonging in the long run to their mother's family—their matrilineage, or abusua. By contrast, the children of a free man and a woman of slave status belonged to their father. Thus it is no wonder that a particular kind of marriage between enslaved women and their masters—called *afona awadie* marriages—became increasingly prevalent in this period.

Enslaved women in these kinds of marriages provided other advantages to their male partners. Unlike marriages of free women, afona awadie marriages did not require the man to make the payments of ritual bride wealth known as the "knocking fee" and the "head fee." These payments, typically made to the family of the bride, were expensive. By the 1870s, "knocking fee" and "head fee" payments together were probably higher than the price of purchasing a female slave. Additionally, wives in the Gold Coast generally possessed many protections, include the right to divorce husbands who mistreated them or did not provide for them. These protections were guaranteed by their families, to whom they could (and often did) flee when unhappy.[8] They could usually take their children with them if they did choose to leave. Slaves, by contrast, enjoyed none of these protections, partly because they did not belong within a local matrilineage or family. They could not divorce their owners, could not flee if mistreated, could not demand the resources and contributions that most husbands had

---

7   Donna J. E. Maier, "Precolonial Palm Oil Production and Gender Division of Labor in Nineteenth-Century Gold Coast and Togoland," *African Economic History*, 37 (2009), 1–32.

8   The best evidence we have for this comes partly from oral histories conducted in Asante at a later date, in the superb volume by Victoria B. Tashjian and Jean Allman, *I Will Not Eat Stone: A Women's History of Colonial Asante* (Portsmouth, NH: Heinemann, 2000).

a duty to provide their wives, and had no real control over their children. As a result, they were in a very different position from most wives.

Yet there is some evidence (as we will discuss below) that some women in afona awadie marriages managed to claim certain rights as wives, despite the fact that they were also slaves. The two conditions were not entirely mutually exclusive, as Abina makes clear in her description of her relationship with Yaw. Two important objects that demonstrate the connection between gender and enslavement, and that also feature in Abina's story, are beads and cloth. These are two real, physical types of objects, but they are also symbols laden with meaning. The significance of the beads, which were cut away from Abina's body by Yaw, is discussed by both Kwasi Konadu and Sandra Greene in their contribution to this volume, below. But it is worth saying a few words about the cloth that Quamina Eddoo allegedly gave to Abina (and the cloth that Tandoe tried to give to her).

Providing cloth was one obligation of husbands to their wives. It was also a duty of fathers for their children—and, it turns out, cloth was one of the items usually provided to slaves by their masters. In all of these situations, gifts of cloth were not merely material transfers but also connoted the establishment of a relationship. In Abina's case, however, a key complication was that both Eddoo and Tandoe gave her cloth, with Tandoe later being reprimanded by Eddoo for having made this gift. How should we understand this transaction? One explanation is that in giving Abina gifts, Eddoo was asserting his authority over Abina. While Tandoe clearly saw himself in the position of the prospective groom and thus believed that he should give these ritual gifts to his promised bride-to-be, the fact that Eddoo berated him for doing so shows that Eddoo believed that he, ultimately, was the individual with authority over Abina. This evidence does go some distance toward suggesting that Eddoo had purchased Abina, as she had claimed.

The pattern of male masters (like Yaw and Quamina Eddoo) and enslaved females (like Abina) was probably typical in this area and time. However, it was clearly not the only model in the region. For one thing, many slaves—albeit a minority—were male. Moreover, there is interesting evidence, put forward by the Ghanaian scholar Kwabena Adu-Boahen, that there were many female slave owners in the Fante region (around Cape Coast) between 1807 and 1874.[9] Some of these women were of Euro-African descent, connected via their fathers to trans-Atlantic trade in palm oil and other goods. They included Mary Barnes and Elizabeth Swanzy,

---

9 Kwabena Adu-Boahen, "Abolition, Economic Transition, Gender and Slavery: The Expansion of Women's Slaveholding in Ghana, 1807–1874," *Slavery and Abolition*, 31 (2010), 117–136.

whose names connect them to two of the largest trading firms in the region. Some of them may have held title to slaves that really belonged to their male partners who were British, and thus not allowed to legally own slaves after 1807. Others were connected to royal families in the region. Female slave owners appear to have been less likely to own large palm oil plantations, and more likely to employ their captives as hawkers and artisans and in farming foodstuffs for sale in town markets such as in Cape Coast and Elmina. Unfortunately, there is not sufficient evidence at this time to know whether the conditions of servitude for women enslaved by other women differed from those who were enslaved by men.

COLONIAL PATERNALISM

Evidence of the connection between gender and enslavement in the nineteenth-century Gold Coast helps us to understand the way that constructions of gender were used to create and enforce relationships of dominance and power. Specifically, slavery in this place and time enforced the power of one sex (male) over another (female). After 1874, this pattern was reinforced by formal British colonialism since in British society, as well, the construction of gender operated to strengthen the power of men over women. The overwhelming way this power was expressed was through the concept of **paternalism**.

Paternalism is the idea that men should organize and manage a society in the same way that fathers should play a leading role in their families. However, each society has its own particular notion of what it means to be a father. In the nineteenth-century British sense of the word, fathers were expected to protect their families, provide for them, but also discipline them if they strayed from the proper, moral path. This meant that the male heads of families generally had expansive rights to punish their spouses and children. This notion was widely embraced, and had implications at the individual level—for example, unlike in Akan society, the children of a marriage were deemed to belong to their fathers—and beyond. In general, British men of the middle and upper classes believed they had the right and the duty to act as fathers to the lower social classes, to women, and to the populations of the colonies.

Thus, in the dominant British colonial conception of the world, it was natural for the family, the state, and indeed the empire to be run by "father" figures whose duty it was to both protect their children/wards/women and to also make decisions for them.[10] This value operated across the empire, and it was present in colonial courtrooms like the one in which Abina

---

10   Philippa Levina, *Gender and Empire* (Oxford: Oxford University Press, 2004).

testified. For example, Melton (and many other British magistrates) frequently accepted the arguments that alleged slaves were in fact the wives, adopted children, or other wards of powerful or rich local men. Melton was generally willing to believe that it was quite natural that women and children should be under the authority of an important adult male. Other magistrates in Cape Coast Colony were willing to accept that violence against the enslaved was better interpreted as the punishment of unruly children. Of course, their willingness to accept this violence had limits. One of the values of Victorian-era paternalism was the belief that father figures should not overly physically abuse or have sexual access to their wards and children. Thus, charges of rape or violent sexual abuse sometimes brought down the wrath of British magistrates on alleged slave owners in the Gold Coast.

Paternalism also influenced the way that colonial administrators allowed some locals to influence the governing of the Colony and Protectorate. Colonialism largely took the form of an alliance between European men and a select group of African men. In the process by which men formulated colonial rule, women gradually lost many of the institutions and beliefs that protected them. One way in which this diminution occurred was that if female slaves wished to take up the opportunity of emancipation, they often could do so only if they gave up rights to their children, regardless of whether their enslaver was the children's biological father. These realities were very much a part of the operation of British colonialism in the Gold Coast, but it is important to note that they often merely exacerbated male power over women that already had a long history in Akan society.[11]

MARRIAGE AND RESPECTABILITY

This book is built around an investigation of Abina Mansah's status as a *slave*. That construction is probably appropriate. After all, it honors Abina's claim to have been enslaved, which brought her to court in the first place. Yet Abina also claims a different status at many points during her testimony—that of a *married woman*. She raises the issue numerous times, both in her assertion that Yaw married her and in her account of the demand that she marry Tandoe. One way—possibly the most important way—of gendering our interpretation of Abina's experiences is therefore to look at Abina's claim to be enslaved through the lens of marriage as well.

---

11   Stefano Boni, "Twentieth-Century Transformations in Notions of Gender, Parenthood, and Marriage in Southern Ghana: A Critique of the Hypothesis of 'Retrograde Steps' for Akan Women," *History in Africa*, 28 (2001), 15–21.

As we saw in the last few sections, marriage and slavery were quite closely related types of relationships in the nineteenth-century Gold Coast. In fact, Abina was not the only woman whose courtroom testimony in this period brought together claims of enslavement with narratives of marriage.[12] Thus, exploring Abina's allegations that she had been enslaved in the context of her claims to be a married woman may also give us insight into the experiences as and actions of a wider group of women as well.

Marriage brought many advantages to a woman in Akan society. Husbands were obliged to provide certain goods including meat and clothing to their wives, and to shelter them. They were also supposed to take up protections initially provided to girls by their fathers, not only physical— from the advances of other men—but also mystical and spiritual. In fact, because Akan speakers largely believed that spiritual well-being was connected to physical welfare, these two kinds of protections were connected. Adult women without husbands did not have these protections. In fact, the importance placed on marriage by Akan society can be demonstrated by proverbs such as "A woman's glory [what causes her to be respected] is her marriage" and "If a woman has no man, then we beat her and swagger."[13] Such proverbs, probably used in everyday speech, arguably helped to promote particular shared ideas and police behavior about gender, relationships, and other ways of acting, although how exactly we should understand them remains highly debated.

Marriage provided both material protections for a woman and, equally importantly, respectability. By contrast, enslaved women did not enjoy many of the protections extended to a wife. Although being attached to a powerful man (or even woman) still might offer some security, it did not offer quite the same spiritual advantages and physical protections. This difference may help us to explain Abina's greatest complaint that as a slave, she "could not look after [her] body and health." More important, perhaps, being a slave was associated not with respectability but rather with shame. Proverbs suggest that slaves were normally forbidden to eat the best palm nuts or dress like wealthier individuals, and were told not to talk about their origins. Moreover, they were exposed to ridicule, as this proverb illustrates: "When your father's slave cuts down a tree you say: 'The wood is soft.'"

Women in afona awadie marriages were both slaves and wives. Thus they existed somewhere in a continuum between exploitation and

---

12 Other such cases from the same period include SCT 5/4/18, *Eccoah Fumah v. Yaw Aboah*, 28 December 1874; SCT 2/4/12, *Regina v. Tintintang & Atoobi*, 15 July 1878; SCT 2/5/1, *Regina v. Okaneley and Quartey*, 5 November 1879.

13 About 7,000 proverbs were collected by Peggy Appiah, Kwame Anthony Appiah, and Ivor Agyeman-Duah in *Bu Me Bε : Proverbs of the Akans* (Oxfordshire, UK: Ayebia Clark, 2007).

protection, between shame and respectability. There is evidence from court cases and also missionary's reports that many women tried to move along this continuum and to become recognized more as wives than as slaves. Abina Mansah might have been attempting just such a move in the court case described in this book. By arguing that she was not only enslaved but also more properly Yaw Awoah's wife, Abina made a powerful case that she should be seen by the administration and by the community as a respectable woman. This may very well have been a primary motive for her decision to go to court.

Go back and reread that last paragraph. It may be the most important revision in this second edition. It shows how looking at this history through a filter of gender reveals new aspects to Abina's purpose and her life experiences as well as those of other women like her. As an example, this revision also demonstrates the broader value of gendering historical studies.

WAS ABINA A SLAVE?

Abina's attempts to be considered a married woman bring into question the label we have used throughout this whole book in describing her as a slave. Despite their usefulness, identity labels like *slave* are troubling, for they threaten to reduce an individual's life to a single dimension. Reducing Abina to her condition of enslavement thus threatens to undercut the project of appreciating the complexity and richness of her life. The label contains another problem as well, for the frame of *slavery* is one that comes from the British colonial project. We have already seen that the Akan categories that might be translated as slavery, such as *odonko* and *awowa*, were not precisely the same as the conditions and status that the term *slavery* conjures up in our minds. Similarly, Abina's life experiences and those of men and women like her never fit well in Melton's categorization and formula of slavery.

These complex issues underpin the question of whether we should label Abina Mansah a slave. The question also raises a more fundamental issue: whether Quamina Eddoo was guilty of purchasing and owning Abina or whether—as both he and his sister allege—she was simply a guest staying in their home at the request of Yaw Awoah.

Because these are complex, entangled issues, they deserve the attention of scholars looking at the question from a multitude of perspectives. In the sections below, three celebrated scholars discuss whether or not Abina was a slave through paradigms that they think are meaningful to anyone reading the story of this incredible woman. Note that, in the spirit of history as a forum, these scholars do not always agree with our interpretation, or with one another!

SANDRA GREENE

Sandra Greene is a professor of history at Cornell University, where she focuses on research and teaching in the field of West African history at the intersection of belief systems, gender, and slavery. One of her books, West African Narratives of Slavery: Texts from Late Nineteenth- and Early Twentieth-Century Ghana (2011), *is among the most important volumes ever published for understanding how enslaved West Africans described their captivity. Her work on the Ewe-speaking people, among whom Abina Mansah may have begun her life, helps her to bring a special perspective to Abina's story.*

WHO WAS ABINA MANSAH?

From the surviving testimony of the 1876 court case *Regina v. Quamina Eddoo,* and from the analysis of this testimony by Trevor Getz, it is clear that Abina Mansah was a very strong-willed young woman. When she found herself seemingly transferred without her knowledge from one man, Yaw Awoah, who had bought her in Adansi, to another, Quamina Eddoo of Salt Pond, who then attempted to force her to marry yet another man, Tandoe, she objected. She fled to the British-controlled town of Cape Coast and sought help. She did not wish to marry a man not of her own choosing, and she did not want to continue to have no "will of [her] own [to control her] body and health." But information contained in the court transcript reveals more than just this. In her testimony, Abina describes herself as more than a slave. She also claims a past. She indicates that she was born in Krepi (the Ewe-speaking area to the east of the Volta River), that she had been captured in war by the Asante general Adu Bofo, that she had remained as his enslaved prisoner of war, and that had been punished by him for "misconduct" until she was sold to another in Adansi.

This testimony—limited as it is—is quite important for understanding who Abina Mansah was. An investigation of the few names and events she mentions can reveal a wealth of information about her and her experiences. She recalls, for example, that it was an Asante general Adu Bofo who captured her during a war. Adu Bofo, was indeed an Asante military commander. In 1869, he crossed the Volta River and attacked the many communities (most of which were Ewe-speaking) that had long resisted the imperial power of Asante. The devastation he and his army wrought resulted in widespread famine and massive casualties, as noted by the German and Swiss missionaries who had been living and working in the area:

> No writing instrument can describe how the Ashante people plague the people here. First, they took everything that the earth had produced so that we already suffer here from dire hunger. . . . The city was looted just as the land had been.[i]

> [On traveling through the region], we often encountered the extremely sad traces of the battle that had taken place the day before: the wounded, the dead, heads separated from torsos, corpses without heads: what a sight![ii]

In 1871, at the end of his military campaign, Adu Bofo moved hundreds of captured men, women, and children in a forced march to the Asante capital of Kumase, well over 100 miles away, which took as long as six months.[iii] By the time they arrived at a village in the vicinity of Kumase, many were barely alive, as noted by a Swiss missionary who himself had been captured:

> [I]n a yard [in a village just outside Kumase, were] more than a hundred prisoners from Krepe, men, women and children, all living skeletons and infants on their mothers' backs, starving for want of their natural nourishment. . . . [P]risoners continued to arrive. The sight of one poor boy touched us deeply; the thin neck was unable to support the head, which drooped almost to the knees. I spoke to him repeatedly, and offered him food; at length he gave me a look I shall never forget and just said, "I have eaten," and the head hung down helpless as before; all hope seemed gone.[iv]

---

i   *Monatsblatt der Norddeutschen Missions-Gesellschaft*, 20, no. 239 (1870), 1082.

ii   F. A. Ramseyer and J. A. Kühne, *Four Years in Ashantee* (New York: Robert Carter and Bros., 1875), 30.

iii   This time calculation of six months is based on a rough estimate from the experience of Aaron Kuku, who was also captured by Asante forces in early 1870, but not moved to Kumase until the middle of that year. See Sandra E. Greene, *West African Narratives of Slavery: Texts from Late Nineteenth- and Early Twentieth-Century Ghana* (Bloomington: Indiana University Press, 2011), 48.

iv   Ramseyer and J. A. Kühne, *Four Years*, 81, 83.

In Kumase, Adu Bofo presented those who survived the march to his king as evidence of the success of his military campaign. Some of these Ewe-speaking captives were immediately executed as an offering to the gods that had brought the Asante army home with such abundant booty. Others, however, were dispersed as war captives, to become the slaves of the various military commanders and subordinates who had supported or participated in the war.[v] Abina appears to have been one of these Ewe-speaking captives. Her testimony indicates how such fragmentary information—her reference to Adu Bofo as her first master in Asante, and her claim to have been born in Krepi—can be used to unearth additional sources that help us obtain a much fuller understanding of who she was and what she experienced.

Her capture and enslavement in Asante was only the beginning of a longer journey for Abina Mansah. After spending some time as Adu Bofo's slave, she was sold to another in Adansi. And in Adansi, she was sold yet again to Yaw Awoah. We can assume that Yaw bought her expecting to reap a number of benefits. He could use her labor, as he probably did when she traveled with him from Adansi to Salt Pond. It was extremely common for traders like Yaw Awoah, to purchase slaves to carry their trade goods when traveling to the coast. On arrival at their destination, they often sold both their goods and those slaves they no longer needed or wanted. The proceeds from these sales would then be used by the trader to purchase additional goods to be sold in the interior.

This certainly seems to be how Yaw Awoah handled his purchase of Abina Mansah. He bought her in Adansi, then traveled with her (presumably loaded with goods) to Salt Pond. He then sold both his goods and her to buyers on the coast. Abina was of more value to Yaw Awoah than simply as a laborer, however. Not only could she work, she could also provide sexual companionship for as long, or for as short, a period as he wished. According to the testimony by both Abina and Adjuah N'Yamiwhah, Yaw Awoah purchased Abina to be both his slave and his wife. Abina then verified several times that Yaw Awoah was indeed also her husband.

What are we to make of this particular claim? Marriage between a man and a woman in nineteenth-century southern Ghana would have normally involved negotiations between the families of the prospective groom and the prospective bride. The families would have had to agree to the marriage and would have sealed that agreement with an exchange of gifts, some of which would have gone to the prospective bride. Only then would the couple have been allowed to engage in sexual relations to consummate the marriage. Failure to engage in these kinds of negotiations before sexual

---

v   For a more complete discussion of how other individual Ewe-speaking peoples experienced this war, see Greene, *West African Narratives*, especially Parts 1 and 2.

intercourse could land a young man in difficulty with the law. The charge: theft. Access to a young woman's sexuality was overseen by her legal male guardian. It was this guardian who would demand compensation for sexual access (i.e., "marriage") to any young woman under his authority. If a man failed to engage in negotiations and compensate this guardian before engaging in intercourse with the young woman, his act was considered to be theft. The guardian had to be compensated.[vi]

None of this, however, applied to Abina. She had been ripped from her home community, forcibly separated from her natal family and thrust into slavery, alone and in a foreign community. Her "marriage" included no negotiations between her family and that of Yaw Awoah. There was no exchange of gifts, no compensation. Rather, Yaw Awoah bought Abina from her previous owner. Whatever negotiations may have occurred involved only discussions between Yaw Awoah and her former master about her purchase price. Upon buying her, it was Yaw Awoah who controlled access to her sexuality. According to Asante law—and because he was also not related to her by blood—he was acting within his rights to engage in sexual relations with her. It was this act that made Abina his "wife." Yaw Awoah claims he paid an elderly relative "head-money," i.e., bride wealth, for his wife. We do not know who this elderly relative was, however, or whether or not his testimony is even true. What is clear is that he did indeed claim Abina as his wife by acknowledging publicly that he had had sexual relations with her. Such a public claim, however, did not require him to alter his understanding of his wife as also his slave. He could still do what he wanted with her.

Slave owners in West Africa were well aware, of course, that their control of those they owned was not absolute. Enslaved individuals had their own feelings and interests, and these sentiments could either undermine the master's own interests or be harnessed in support of them. Several proverbs from the Asante and Fante areas speak to this very understanding:

1. A servant is like . . . corn ground into flour; when a little water is sprinkled on it, it becomes soft.
2. Even if your mother's son is "Kubuobi" [i.e., an *odonko*, a slave] would you tell him that the big drum was a fit thing for him to carry?[vii]

---

vi   R. S. Rattray, *Religion and Art in Ashanti* (London: Oxford University Press, 1927), 78, 78n1.

vii   These two proverbs can be found in R. Sutherland Rattray, *Ashanti Proverbs: The Primitive Ethics of a Savage People* (London: Oxford University Press, 1916), 122, 128.

Knowing that it was in the interest of slave owners to manipulate the feelings and interests of their slaves for their own benefit, how might we understand the relationship that is said to have existed between Yaw Awoah and Abina? As a symbol of their ties to one another, Abina and Yaw Awoah both acknowledged that he gave her beads, which she wore around her leg. This might suggest, again, that the beads were Yaw's public acknowledgment of his marriage to Abina. Yet Yaw still sold Abina to Quamina Eddoo. Was the gift simply a ruse to get Abina to be a more compliant slave? Did Yaw Awoah give beads to Abina as a way to "sprinkle water on ground corn to soften it"—that is, to calm her, to make her more controllable? After all, she had already suffered horrific experiences on being enslaved and marched to Asante. She then suffered beatings while enslaved by Adu Bofo, and was then sold unceremoniously by Adu Bofo to her new owner in Adansi, and from this owner to Yaw Awoah, who then sexually imposed himself on her. Did he publicly acknowledge her as his wife and give her beads to encourage her to be more accepting of her situation? Did Abina then realize his lack of sincerity when they reached Salt Pond when he then sold her to Quamina Eddoo and removed the beads he had given her? Did Abina then use Yaw Awoah's public acknowledgment that she was his wife, even after she thought he had sold her to Quamina Eddoo, because this was the only way she could fend off yet another "marriage" to Eddoo's slave, Tandoe?

The testimony provides us with few answers to these questions. What we do know is that Abina Mansah was a very strong-willed woman. After having been captured during Asante's wars east of the Volta River, she—and thousands of other men, women, and children—suffered both starvation and the devastating loss of friends, neighbors, and relatives. Relocated to Kumase following a forced march of several months spanning more than 100 miles, she found herself alone and enslaved in a foreign land, passed from one owner to another, beaten, chained to a log, and unable to exercise control over her own body or health. She did not succumb, however. Instead, she fled to Cape Coast and sought her freedom. Determined not to hide in fear after escaping from her master, convinced of the righteousness of her case, she took her case to court.

KWASI KONADU

Kwasi Konadu is among the most skilled and significant historians of the Akan-speaking peoples of Ghana at work today. His recent book The Akan Diaspora in the Americas *(OUP, 2012) has been enormously influential in uncovering cultural patterns and ideas that were deeply embedded in Akan society and how they have changed over time. His contribution to this debate demonstrates the value of this information, helping us to interpret the transcript in terms of Akan cultural institutions and symbols that come through in the testimony of Abina and others. The spellings of names and the characters "ɔ" and "ɛ" used in the Twi proverbs below are both introduced on page xix.*

WAS ABINA MANSAH A "SLAVE"?

In many ways all historians are captives to a foreign territory called the past and to the sources that provide the means of transport to its times, places, and peoples. Historians have thus been equally captivated by stories such as Abina Mansah but also constrained by the very two-dimensional documents where Abina's voice appears in third person and where that voice was translated from a local idiom into a language as foreign to Abina as the past is to most of us. That said, how do we make sense of the ultimately Indo-European term *slave* in the case of this young Akan woman named Abina Mansah (*Abena*—Tuesday-born female; *Mansa*—third-born female child) and in broader human history? And, more specifically, was Abina a "slave" in her own time and land of origin?

In the only recovered sources for Abina's story, the main character makes a number of claims that, taken together, may help to answer these questions.[i] According to the court transcript, in which Abina's voice

---

i   On the question of sources and African understandings of their own enslavement, see Kwasi Konadu, *Transatlantic Africa, 1440–1888* (New York: Oxford University Press, 2014), esp. the introduction and Chapters 1 and 4.

intermittently appears, Abina claims to be the wife of a merchant named Yaw Awoah, whom she views as both husband and "master," though she also called "master" the acting judicial assessor W. Melton or any (British colonial) "white man," suggesting power over people was central to her understanding of her shifting status. Purportedly, on news of a dying brother in the forested Asante region, Yaw leaves his "wife" Abina with "important man" Quamina Eddoo (Kwamina Edu), who makes Abina live with his sister Eccoah Coom (Ekua Kuma) and soon tells Abina she was given in marriage to one of his servants (and former captive), Tandoe. Abina views this forced marriage as a financial transaction— "I thought that I had been sold"—and her acceptance of two pieces of cloth, and perhaps the handkerchief from Tandoe, confirmed in her mind, "I had been purchased." But if the cloth transaction was tied to marriage, and the threat of violence when she refused to be married induced her to run away, was she really seeking "freedom" from "slavery" or from a coerced marriage?

Up until now in the story, Abina seems more concerned with her status as "wife" (Twi: *oyere*) than as a "slave." Abina tells us Yaw Awoah, at the time of his departure, removed and took with him in remembrance only the beads below her knee, likely her ankle, and not her waist beads, whereas Kwamina Edu orders his male servants to cut off Abina's waist beads at the pronouncement of the forced marriage. The beads tell an important story. In Akan culture, both women and men adorn themselves with beads, but specific kinds of precious beads, beyond pure aesthetics, mark significant rites of passage in life, such as birth and puberty. The Akan have puberty rites, but only for young girls; these rites typically begin at the onset of the first menstrual cycle and are geared primarily toward marriage and motherhood. Including lessons about taking care of one's body, health and family, these rites also include the acquisition of precious beads (e.g., *bodom*) that punctuate the transition to womanhood, protect and preserve that womanhood, and serve as markers of socioeconomic status. Only the husband is allowed to see the waist beads of a married woman. The cutting and removal of Abina's waist beads represented a severance from her "marriage" to Yaw Awoah and a greater loss of control over her body and female sexuality, since it is the imposition of a new husband (Tandoe) upon Abina that provoked her numerous use of the phrase "my own" in reference to her "(free) will" and her "body."

The salience of marriage more than the binary notions of "slavery" and "freedom" is also confirmed by Abina's own refracted words. Abina tells us she was a captive in the Asante areas of Kumase and Adansi where she accepted her status and where she was first a captive of one

Adu Bofo[ii] and that her treatment or work regiment in the Asante region and in Saltpond were essentially the same (with the exception of the flogging and logging in Asante). But, fully cognizant of her status as captive in the Asante region, why didn't Abina run away earlier? The answer lies in the fact that the Asante region was outside the legal (colonial) jurisdiction of the British "protected" territories and so running away was a political dead end. But, more important, the answer also lies in matrimony. Marriage to Yaw Awoah, whether real or imagined, offered some protection from the physical and verbal abuse that afflicted Abina's young female co-captives (Akosua, Abena, Adwoa, and Ama); it gave some value to her labor (Abina complained her laboring for Ekua was without compensation); and, central to understanding Abina's social world was that marriage was assimilative, it incorporated those on the fringes of "free" society and offered the possibility of "free" status to the children of servile women. Birth and marriage are the most fundamental ways to enter a family or lineage; a childbearing young woman like Abina would have seized these fundamental opportunities of marriage and childbirth to become linked with "free" men like Yaw Awoah in order to stabilize her shifting status from captive to wife to stranger-captive and to enjoy some of the greater female autonomy Akan women typically exercised through maternal responsibility in matrilineal Akan societies.

So, was Abina Mansah a "slave"? The better questions are, *when* was Abina a "slave," and how did her shifting status matter for a fuller grasp of African and global slaveries? Insights into these broader questions lie in Akan social categories as they existed between the ages of transatlantic slaving and abolition and as revealed by the court transcript. In Akan society, the terms *akoa* ("subject"), *odonkɔ* ("enslaved person of northern [Ghana] origins"), and *awowa* ("pawn"; person given as surety for the debt of a kin) were dynamic, and played key roles in assimilating a newly enslaved person into his or her host society. Pawnage and judicial punishment were ways in which an Akan could be enslaved—even debtors sometimes pawned themselves. Such forms of social domination existed in the Asante region where Abina was captured and exchanged at least twice in the late nineteenth century. Moreover, as the growth of large-scale plantation laboring around Kumase ended, the scope of domestic forms of social servitude, such as pawnage, increased the numbers of unfree persons in Akan households even as the descendants of *odonkɔ* were assimilated into the Akan matrilineal society. Those enslaved and of foreign or northern origin

---

ii   Or Bafo, or Bɔfoɔ.

could receive full membership within a family after a generation and personal property rights and some authority were extended to them and their descendants—safeguarded by the taboo against questioning one's origins or his/her servile past.[iii]

In the court transcript, Ekua Kuma was asked if Abina was treated as a guest, servant, slave, or stranger. Though these are just some of the major social markers of belonging and marginality, and with their own degrees of rights and obligations, they tell us much. A guest was a visitor of almost any rank, standing, or culture; servants could be captives but were also socioeconomically distinct from "slaves" though both often did the same kind of work; and a stranger, a sociocultural category, could be either of the above and more. Abina was referred to as a stranger/slave, confirming her servile and outsider status. Viewed from Abina's perspective, marriage to Yaw would have addressed her mutually reinforcing statuses, since the servile-outsider was a kinless (adult) stranger who could be brought into lineage membership and possibly receive the corporate protection thereof only through marriage. To this, the Akan say, *ɔhɔhoɔ te sɛ abofra* ("The stranger is like a child") and *ɔhɔhoɔ ani kɛsee na nso ɔnhunu kuro mu* ("The stranger has big eyes yet s/he doesn't know his/her whereabouts in town"). The stranger, like the child or servile wife, is both vulnerable and dependent and thus is thought to need paternalistic guidance and protection. Abina would have been no different, as borne out by her story. In the end, Abina is discharged by the acting judicial assessor and is legally "free." But she probably remained in the British protectorate as a sociocultural stranger among largely Fante and British norms, kinless and with a servile past, and likely sought out marriage rather than some vague idea of emancipation to counter the jagged and incongruous forces of freedom and abolition, Christianity and commerce, and imperialism and "civilization" operating in the late nineteenth-century world.

---

iii   On these matters, see Kwasi Konadu, "Euro-African Commerce and Social Chaos: Akan Societies in the Nineteenth and Twentieth Centuries," *History in Africa*, 36, no. 1 (2009), 265–292.

ANTOINETTE BURTON

Antoinette Burton is a historian and prodigious author who works at the intersection of empire and gender. Abina's story resonates with her work for many reasons. As a world historian, she has promoted a "world history from below" approach that emphasizes the significance of individual and collective human stories. As an innovative teacher, she brings a critical approach to pedagogy that supports experiments such as this volume. Most important, perhaps, her work, including the now-classic edited volume Bodies in Contact: Rethinking Colonial Encounters in World History (2005), *reveals the way that the physical body was a site of contact and interaction in colonial settings. In her contribution, she shows the way that sexuality and the body play into the question of whether Abina was, or should be, described as a slave.*

SEX AND SLAVERY IN THE 1876 CASE OF ABINA MANSAH

The slice of Abina Mansah's story that we get from the 1876 transcript raises more questions than answers—which makes it the perfect text for testing a number of hypotheses. Surely the question of whether or not Abina was a slave is the most challenging one. Paradoxically, even those who acknowledged that Quamina Eddoo was her "master" said no. According to his sister Eccoah Coom's testimony, he never compelled her to do work; he never gave her any cloths; and he never called her a slave. Eccoah denies outright that Abina was a slave of her brother, claiming she was merely a servant of her brother's friend. In fact, she repeatedly denies the legal relationship of slave by substituting a more casual set of connections and insisting that Abina was no relation: nothing more than a stranger to her. In doing so she tries to sidestep both the category and the charge of slaveholder for Quamina Eddoo and, by extension, his whole family as well. Eccoah works hard, in other words, to evacuate Eddoo's relationship with Abina of power so that he will appear innocent of the charge of "slave dealing."

Abina, on the other hand, tries to show the court that she was bound to her master despite denials to the contrary. Her evidence reads like a point-counterpoint: yes, he coerced her labor; yes, she was given to him by Yowawah as a slave; and yes, both Yowawah and Eccoah are making false statements. Though no one else in the transcript mentions it, for Abina the question of sex is part of the argument about whether or not she was a slave. Her question to Yowawah, "On the night when you went and left me with Eddoo did you call me to sleep with you?" may suggest that for her, Yowawah's demand is proof of her bondage to him. In an all-too-familiar case of he said/she said, he denies that he made any such claim. The court rejects Abina's charge against Eddoo, but in the end Yowawah himself is accused and charged of dealing with, holding, and treating her as a slave. That case is shortly thrown out, leaving Abina presumably without recourse.

The testimonies of all the parties suggest that everyone involved understood what slavery was: legally sanctioned power over another person, the exercise of which denies the slave her own sovereignty. For Abina, that sovereignty was embodied as well as gendered. Its violation was not simply a legal matter but an intimate one as well. To be sure, freedom means mobility and the capacity to work if not exactly at what one chooses, then at least of one's own volition. But we might wonder whether Abina raises the question of Yowawah's demand that she sleep with him to represent her conviction that a man's power over a woman's body is a sign of his dominion and, therefore, of her slavery.

Here we have to remember the conditions under which the transcript was produced and Abina's testimony translated. This seems especially germane in light of how delicate it would have been in any nineteenth-century courtroom, practically the world over, to have a woman testifying about sexual demands made of her, even in the context of conjugal relations. Certainly this was true for white women; the mere mention of sex by a woman in a public place was enough to throw her reputation as a respectable woman into question; and the distance between "unrespectable" women and prostitutes in this period was very slight indeed. We know that in the context of British imperialism, the sexuality of African women was viewed very differently, at least by white men, who considered African women to be sexually available—and therefore to be incapable of being respectable—as a matter of course. It's impossible to determine from the transcript what Eddoo, Yowawah, or James Brew made of Abina's question about sexual relations. Perhaps they were content to have her endanger her respectability, hoping it would help Eddoo's case. Or perhaps they were simply confident that the law would protect them even and especially with respect to the question of a husband's customary right to sexual relations. If it was a risk to Abina's credibility to ask her question, this may suggest how key she believed it was to the matter of whether or not she was a slave. And if James Davis prompted her on this subject, it might have been because he understood that in the context of slavery, there could be some sympathy for Abina's helplessness in the face of coercion in matters of sex. This would probably have required him to know something about the history of metropolitan sentiment about slavery and abolition, which represented enslaved women as objects of pity in need of humanitarian intervention.

What else would *we* need to know to answer these questions definitively? Ideally, we'd need more knowledge of how the men involved viewed their relationships with the women they took as wives and how those women balanced household life, childrearing and the beginnings of market-based participation in the local economy. Anthropologists like Gracia Clark have been able to get at these questions for the twentieth century. Her fieldwork yielded evidence that wives' independence within marriage was rated as a "virtue" by trader husbands in and around Kumasi and that "Asante women value sexual satisfaction and companionship within marriage, although they seem to consider reliable financial support more essential and more likely."[i] Unfortunately, such evidence is harder, if not impossible, to obtain for Abina's time because oral histories from that period do not exist. Historians like Jean Allman and Victorian Tashjian used recollections of Asante women born between 1900 and 1925 to try to understand how they negotiated the shifting economic and social landscape of their time.[ii] Alas, Abina was born well before their study, which gives us insight into several generations beyond her lifetime but leaves us wondering about what parallels with her experience there might have been.

Though these works cannot shed direct light on Abina's claim to be a slave, they remind us that later West African women moved beyond the dilemmas she faced and into a marketplace where they found some more consonance, it would seem, between their personal lives and their working lives. To be sure, they too lived under British rule and local male leadership; their lives were not necessarily easier, we just know more about them. Meanwhile, as a strategy, Abina's decision to cite her sexual obligation to Yowawah served her no better than her other claims against

---

i   Gracia Clark, *Onions Are My Husband: Survival and Accumulation by West African Market Women* (Chicago: University of Chicago Press, 1994), pp. 338–339.

ii Jean Allman and Victorian Tashjian, *"I Will Not Eat Stone": A Women's History of Colonial Asante* (Portsmouth, NH: Heinemann, 2000).

Eddo. Whether it tipped the scales against Yowawah is hard to say (and as mentioned above, his indictment didn't stick in any case). Yet Abina's invocation of the demand of sex is trace evidence not just of *whether* the fact of slavery mattered to her but of *how* it did as well. We cannot assume anything about what the sexual act meant to Abina emotionally or psychologically or spiritually—or, for that matter, to Yowawah or Eddoo either. The transcript can tell us only so much. It may indicate that the demand for sexual favors was one of several forms of "power over" that defined slavery in practice though not in legal terms. If the transcript itself is a staircase of voices, slavery too was a staircase of meanings for Abina and the "important men" with whom, and against whom, she struggled to make her claim. In a court of law, the priority is to win. In this case, the defendants were able to either discredit all of Abina's arguments or trade on the assumption that would be deemed irrelevant. Thus Eddoo and Yowawah evaded the charge of slavery, sexual or otherwise.

READING QUESTIONS

INTRODUCTORY QUESTIONS FOR STUDENTS AT ALL LEVELS

Answer the following questions by focusing on the original transcript and referring when necessary to the graphic interpretation.

1. What questions does Magistrate Melton ask to try to determine whether Abina Mansah was *really* a slave? Why do you think he asks these questions?

2. Why do you think Abina Mansah did not know that Yowahwah had sold her to Quamina Eddoo at first? Why do you think the transaction was hidden from her?

3. Why do you think it is of value for us to learn about people from the past, like Abina Mansah, who weren't important political leaders or leading social or military figures?

4. On the basis of what evidence does Eccoah Coom argue that Abina had not been enslaved by her and her brother Quamina Eddoo?

5. Why do you think Abina Mansah decided to take her former master to court? What was her objective? What evidence from the court transcript supports your interpretation?

The following questions are based largely on the reading guide, although you will find it useful to refer to other sections of the book as well.

6. What was the "civilizing mission," as presented in this volume, and where do we find it in the transcript and graphic history?

7. Consider the idea that the graphic history of Abina is the product of a "staircase" of voices. Whose voices are present in the graphic history? How did each person help to shape and produce it?

8. The transcript of Abina's testimony was intentionally produced. Why do you think such cases were recorded? Who was the intended audience? What message did Melton want them to take away from the transcript?

9. How do the authors try to ensure that the graphic history provides an accurate representation of the place and time in which it is set?

10. Would you consider the Gold Coast okyeame, described in Part IV, a historian? Why, or why not? What is a historian?

QUESTIONS FOR STUDENTS AT THE UNIVERSITY OR COLLEGE LEVEL

Answer the following questions by focusing on the original transcript and referring when necessary to the graphic interpretation.

11. What do the questions Melton asks Abina tell us about his conception of slavery?

12. Read through the trial, and identify points at which Abina Mansah misunderstands, is unable to answer, or contradicts the questions asked by Melton, Davis, and Brew. Why are these moments so important to hearing Abina's perspective? What do they tell us about the different ways in which each participant understood slavery?

13. Consider Abina's statement "If when Yowahwah gave me to defendant to keep the defendant had not given me in marriage to Tandoe I would not have entertained such an idea that I had been sold. *Because defendant gave me in marriage I knew that I had been sold.*" How did Quamina Eddoo's actions in giving Abina to Tandoe in marriage alert her to the fact that she had been sold and had the status of a slave in his household?

14. James Davis, who was probably of mixed European and African heritage, acted both as the court interpreter and the defense attorney. In the graphic novel, we represent him as having coached, shaped, or edited Abina Mansah's original statement and testimony. Do you agree? Why, or why not?

15. Davis also represents Abina as having approached him out of the blue, and implies that he had no prior relationship to her, yet we argue that they probably did have a longer relationship. Why do you think we are correct or incorrect on this point?

16. Adjuah N'Yamiwhah's testimony is part of the document that was lost and recently refound. How does her testimony contradict or affirm Abina's? How does it shift the evidence in this case? How does it contribute to our understanding of Abina's life and her experiences in Quamina Eddoo's household?

The following questions are based largely on the reading guide, although you will find it useful to refer to other sections of the book as well.

17. In the reading guide, the "civilizing mission" is exemplified by two quotes—one from the British prime minister Joseph Chamberlain and one from the Sierra Leonean F. Fitzgerald. In the graphic history as well, Brew is depicted as being a believer in the superiority of at least great benefits of British civilization, partly because of statements he made during his career that suggest that he harbored such sentiments. How do you account for the support given by some West Africans in this period for British "civilization" and even British rule in the region?

18. The author argues that Abina managed to overcome the historical "silencing" of people of her class by testifying in court, thus making her voice available to us today. Evaluate this argument. How were people of her class silenced in the period? Does this graphic novel reverse that silencing?

19. How do the author and illustrator read the transcript of Abina's testimony against the grain?

20. What does the author argue is Abina's "truth"? Do you agree or disagree? Why?

21. Although records exist of some 100 or more cases in which allegedly enslaved people testified in late nineteenth-century Gold Coast, Abina's testimony is unique in length and completeness. Can it be said that she is *representative* of a larger group of people, or should we treat her as *exceptional* and unique?

22. One of the measures of whether a historical work is *authentic*, according to the author and illustrator, is the affirmative answer to the question "Would Abina recognize herself in this story?" Is this a useful question for historians to ask themselves in producing a history? Why, or why not?

The following questions are based largely on the "Engaging Abina" section.

23. What does it mean to "gender" Abina's story? How does "gendering" this story allow for new insights into the experiences and perspectives of Abina and other individuals in this story? How does it give us additional insights into the broader experiences and perspectives of groups of people?

24. What is *paternalism*, and how did it operate in the colonial context in which this history is set?

25. How should we understand beads and cloth as evidence of social relationships, and what meanings did they convey in this story?

26. Was Abina a slave? Include a discussion of how the term *slave* should be defined in this context in your answer, and justify your response.

27. Sandra Greene and Kwasi Konadu give varying analyses of Abina's heritage based on either Ewe or Akan origins. Why would her ethnic origins be significant to understanding this story?

28. How does the use of proverbs by the author and by Sandra Greene and Kwasi Konadu contribute to the story? What seem to be their methodologies for using these proverbs? Can proverbs be used in exactly the same way as written sources in the process of historical interpretation? Why or why not?

ADDITIONAL QUESTIONS FOR ADVANCED UNDERGRADUATE AND GRADUATE STUDENTS

Answer the following questions by focusing on the original transcript and referring when necessary to the graphic interpretation.

29. What do the questions Melton asks tell us about his conception of "rights"?

30. Abina Mansah gives a whole series of statements that give us clues as to how it felt to be in her position. Interpret these statements in the context they appear in the testimony. What was Abina Mansah trying to tell the magistrate, and what do these statements tell us about her experiences and perspectives?

    a. "[W]hen a free person is sitting down at ease the slave is working that is what I know."

    b. "I had been sold and I had no will of my own and I could not look after my body and health."

    c. "As they were in defendant's house long before if the defendant had done anything for them I could not tell *but as for me he did nothing good for me.*"

    d. "I thought I was a slave, because when I went for water or firewood I was not paid."

The following questions are based largely on the reading guide, although you will find it useful to refer to other sections of the book as well.

31. Consider the arguments of Hayden White and others that historians merely construct the past based on plots available to them in their own culture. To what degree do you think the interpretation of Abina presented in this volume reflects Abina's "truths," and to what degree do they represent those of the authors and our society today? On what basis can you make this argument?

32. It is possible to suggest that by turning Abina's testimony into a graphic history, the author and historian have become the main voices, effectively marginalizing Abina's own voice in the telling of her story. Do you agree or disagree? Why? Would it have been better to merely present the testimony as is and alone?

33. Some critics have argued that "deconstruction" is at times really "speculation," and that scholars read too much into sources. Can you find instances of speculation in the graphic history that are not sufficiently supported by evidence in the transcript? Is this a problem? Why, or why not?

34. This graphic history can be read as a cultural history of the ideas of four or five individuals. Can it also be said to be a social history? Of whom and what?

35. The author has striven to represent Abina's story in this volume as more of a "forum" than a "temple." Do you think this volume succeeds as a forum? Why, or why not? What are the advantages and disadvantages of this approach?

The following questions are based largely on the "Engaging Abina*" section.*

36. Consider Mitchell's challenge to the author and illustrator to *gender* this story. What was our strategy for doing so, and did we succeed?

37. How does framing this story around *marriage* rather than *slavery* subtly shift the interpretation, and do you agree with the new interpretation that places marriage at the center of the story?

38. How does Antoinette Burton's focus on sexuality and the body relate to the issue of whether or not Abina was a slave? What broader questions does this raise regarding the defining of "slavery"?

TIMELINE

1300 — ca. 1300 First major Akan-speaking state, the kingdom of Bono, forms in the forest region.

1325

1350

1375

1400 — ca. 1441 Atlantic slave trade begins.

1425

1450 — 1471 Portuguese rent land from the ruler of Edina, Kwa Amankwa, to build Elmina Castle. It becomes the first European presence on the Gold Coast.

1475

1500

1525

1550

1575

1600

1600

1610

1620

1630

1640

1650

1660

1670

1680

1690

1700

1710

1720

1730

1740

1750

1760

1770

1780

1790

1800

1640s The town of Cape Coast emerges as a major political and military player in the region as the capital of the state (*oman*) of Fetu.

1650s–1710s Danish, French, British, Dutch, and German merchant companies arrange to lease or buy land, or seize it forcibly, to compete with the Portuguese for control over trade with the region.

1680s–1700s Earliest known *asafo* companies emerge, mostly in the interior but also on the coasts.

1745 Richard Brew, paternal ancestor of James Hutton Brew, arrives in West Africa.

1800

1807 Britain criminalizes the Atlantic slave trade due to pressure from abolitionists, including Afro-Britons like Gustavas Vassa (Olaudah Equiano).

1807 Asante invades the coast, establishing control over most trade between the region and Europe.

1823–1824 Conflict between British and Asante results in the death of Sir Charles Macarthy, reaffirming Asante supremacy in the region.

1834–1835 Slavery is abolished throughout the British Empire.

1843–1844 British and some coastal rulers sign the "Bond of 1844," which formalizes relationships between them.

1850

1865 Administrator Edward Conran exiles the ruler of Cape Coast, Joseph Aggery, effectively imposing direct British rule over the town.

1867–1871 Dutch abandon their forts on the coast, leaving British as sole European power in the region. Citizens of Cape Coast and neighboring states form the Fante Confederation. Leaders include James Hutton Brew.

1873–1874 Anglo-Asante war results in the creation of the Gold Coast Colony and Protectorate.

1875 British antislavery laws are applied in the Gold Coast Colony and Protectorate.

1876 Abina Mansah's case is brought to trial.

1896 A second Anglo-Asante war ends in defeat of Asante armies and the establishment of British control over much of the former Asante state.

1900

1900

1905

1910

1915

1920

1925

1930

1935

1940

1945

1950

1955

1960

1965

1970

1975

1980

1985

1990

1995

2000

1902 British take control of Northern Territories, establishing final boundaries of the Gold Coast Colony.

1925 Constitution of 1925 establishes a "council of chiefs" to advise British governors.

1948 Veterans returning from Second World War march for new rights. Several are shot, and six leaders are detained, giving rise to a mass movement for independence.

1957 British Gold Coast Colony becomes independent state of Ghana.

1979 Cape Coast Castle named a UNESCO World Heritage site.

2011 *Abina and the Important Men* published.

FURTHER RESOURCES

ABINA MANSAH

So far as we can tell, Abina Mansah appears in the official archives of the Republic of Ghana only once—in the old, moldering court documents, book number SCT 5-4-19, case of *Regina* (Queen Victoria) *versus Quamina Eddoo*, 10 Nov 1876, and again a few days later for a final verdict.

Like most other poor Africans who happen to be written into the archives of a colonial court—indeed, like most other poor, "everyday" people in any archive—she was ignored during the period of the great political and economic historians that dominated the last century. When she finally found her way into a scholarly work, it was in a "social history" as, literally, a footnote. I (Trevor) was the author of that social history, *Slavery and Reform in West Africa: Toward Emancipation in Nineteenth-Century Senegal and the Gold Coast* (Athens: Ohio University Press, 2004), and at that stage in my career I was more engaged with putting together evidence about the "experience" of a group of Africans than focusing on the perspective of a few. Abina's case, along with those of other Africans claiming to have been enslaved, supported my wider arguments about social change in the region in the late nineteenth century.

Yet Abina's case was haunting, partly because of her insistence that she be heard in court. Still, the process of understanding what she was saying was difficult, partly because the "important men" in the case were so loud. My first step in excavating her voice was therefore to understand the position and views of men like Melton, a task that culminated in the research and publication of "British Courts, Slave-Owners, and Child Slaves in Post-Proclamation Gold Coast, 1874–1899," in *Child Slaves in the Modern World*, edited by Gwyn Campbell, Suzanne Miers, and Joseph C. Miller (Athens: Ohio University Press, 2010), first written for a 2004 conference in Avignon, France.

I was ready now to write about Abina, but the opportunity really only presented itself when I was invited to a conference put on by four leading scholars of the history of slavery in Africa—Alice Bellagamba, Martin Klein, Sandra Greene, and Carolyn Brown. The conference, titled "Finding the African Voice: Narratives of Slavery," was held in Bellagio, Italy, in 2007. Two volumes have emerged from the conference of collected papers. The first, *African Voices on Slavery and the Slave Trade*, was published in 2011 by Cambridge University Press. This volume reprints Abina's testimony with brief interpretations for students, and includes the article "Interpreting Gold Coast Supreme Court Records, SCT 5/4/19: Regina (Queen) vs. Quamina Eddoo." The second, forthcoming from Africa World Press and provisionally entitled *Looking for the Tracks: Essays on African Sources for the History of Slavery and the Slave Trade*, focuses more on interpretations and includes a chapter that I wrote about the case, "Abina Mansah and the Important Men: Contesting Definitions and Experiences of Enslavement in Post-proclamation Gold Coast Courtrooms."

In 2011, the first edition, *Abina and the Important Men*, was published by Oxford University Press. In 2013 the book won the Best Book for Older Readers award from Africa Access; in 2014 it received the James Harvey Robinson Prize from the American Historical Association. Meanwhile, however, I began to work with Lindsay Ehrisman on gender aspects of the testimony in this case. The results will be published in 2015 in the seminal issue of the *Journal of West African History* as "The Marriages of Abina Mansah—Escaping the Boundaries of 'Slavery' as a Category in Historical Analysis." Gendering Abina's story significantly deepened the analysis of her motives and actions, and those narratives are represented in this second edition of *Abina and the Important Men*.

It is accurate to say that by telling her story in court back in 1876, Abina gave me both inspiration and work. I hope to repay her by retelling her story in this volume to as wide an audience as possible.

SLAVERY AND ABOLITION ON THE GOLD COAST

There are many volumes about slavery and abolition in Africa and elsewhere that deserve mention in this brief bibliography, but I will confine myself to a short discussion of those focusing on the Gold Coast.

Among the superior works on slavery in what is today Ghana are Peter Haenger, *Slaves and Slave Holders on the Gold Coast: Towards an Understanding of Social Bondage in West Africa* (Basel, Switzerland: P. Schlettwein, 2000); Benedict Der, *The Slave Trade in Northern Ghana* (Accra, Ghana: Woeli, 1998); and Akosua Perbi, *A History of Indigenous*

Slavery in Ghana: From the 15th to the 19th Century (Accra, Ghana: Sub-Saharan, 2004).

The debate about abolition on the Gold Coast, specifically, includes a number of articles and books, including Raymond Dumett and Marion Johnson, "Britain and the Suppression of Slavery in the Gold Coast Colony, Ashanti, and the Northern Territories," in *The End of Slavery in Africa*, edited by Suzanne Miers and Richard Roberts (Madison: University of Wisconsin Press, 1988); Gerald McSheffrey, "Slavery, Indentured Servitude, Legitimate Trade, and the Impact of Abolition in the Gold Coast, 1874–1910: A Reappraisal," *Journal of African History*, 24 (1983), 349–68; Kwabena Opare Akurang-Parry, "The Administration of the Abolition Laws, African Response, and Post-proclamation Slavery in the Gold Coast, 1874–1940," *Slavery and Abolition*, 19, no. 2 (1998), 149–66; and Trevor Getz, "The Case for Africans: The Role of Slaves and Masters in Emancipation on the Gold Coast, 1874–2000," *Slavery and Abolition*, 21, no. 1 (2000). A forthcoming anthology on this subject is currently being planned by Rebecca Shumway that will include works from young academics like Steffen Runkel as well as senior scholars like Akosua Perbi.

There are a number of wider studies of slavery in Africa that deserve mention here as well. These include the classics by Paul Lovejoy, *Transformations in Slavery* (Cambridge: Cambridge University Press, 1983); Martin Klein, ed., *Breaking the Chains: Slavery Bondage, and Emancipation in Modern Africa and Asia* (Madison: University of Wisconsin Press, 1993); and Suzanne Miers and Richard Roberts, eds., *The End of Slavery in Africa* (Madison: University of Wisconsin Press, 1988). Others deserve mention, but I will limit myself here to saying that anyone wishing to research further should look at Joseph Miller's fabulous *Slavery and Slaving in World History: A Bibliography—Vol. 2, 1992–96* (Armonk, NY: M. E. Sharpe, 1999) and Sean Stilwell's new *Slavery and Slaving in African History* (Cambridge: Cambridge University Press, 2014).

COLONIALISM AND THE GOLD COAST

There are numerous histories of the Gold Coast, several of which cover the colonial period particularly well. In order of complexity, these include F. K. Buah, *History of Ghana* (London: Macmillan, 1998); and Roger Gocking, *The History of Ghana* (New York: Greenwood Press, 2005).

There are also numerous more specific works that may be of interest to readers. For a gendered history, Victoria B. Tashjian and Jean Allman, *I Will Not Eat Stone: A Women's History of Colonial Asante* (Portsmouth, NH: Heinemann, 2000), is essential. Also recommended from

Africa and the Legacy of Late Colonialism (Princeton, NJ: Princeton University Press, 1996).

GENDER AND AFRICAN HISTORY

For much of the history of History, both women and the paradigm of gender have been largely ignored. It is now widely recognized that this has both limited historians' capacities to understand the past and rendered many of our findings inaccurate. This is nowhere truer than in Africa, where Western historians long ignored the role of gender and the presence of women. Both their assumptions and their ignorance have been overturned in the last quarter century by some very serious scholars. Chief among these are the Nigerians Ifi Amadiume and Oyeronke Oyewumi. Amadiume's *Male Daughters, Female Husbands* (London: Zed Books, 1987) showed the world the ways in which the flexible gender systems of Ibo speakers created a very different reality from those of their British colonial rulers. Oyewumi showed how among the Yoruba, even so basic a category as *woman* is both more complex and more absent than in modern, Western societies in *The Invention of Women* (Minneapolis: University of Minnesota Press, 1997).

The work of scholars like these is chronicled in Nancy Rose Hunt's article "Placing African Women's History and Locating Gender," *Social History*, 14, no. 3 (1989), 359. Since that publication, a generation of scholars has begun to firmly gender the study of the African past in many excellent articles and monographs as well as several superb collected works. Three especially recommended anthologies are Lisa Lindsay and Stephan Miescher, eds., *Men and Masculinities in Modern Africa* (Portsmouth, NH: Heinemann, 2003); Jean Allman, Susan Geiger, and Nakanyike Musisi, eds., *Women in African Colonial Histories*, (Bloomington: Indiana University Press, 2002); and Catherine Cole, Takyiwaa Manuh, and Stephan F. Miescher, eds., *Africa After Gender?* (Bloomington: Indiana University Press, 2007).

WEB RESOURCES

Historians have only belatedly recognized the value of the web both as a research tool and a place to disseminate their findings. Moreover, many of them are still wary of a medium so friendly to disinformation and error. However, there are several web resources that are worth visiting if you are interested in the topics, places, and times discussed in *Abina*.

First, Cape Coast Castle museum has its own website (http://www .capecoastcastlemuseum.com/), which was developed with the assistance of historians and other scholars.

Additionally, readers who are interested in the Atlantic slave trade should look at the website developed by Manu Herbstein to accompany his novel *Ama* (http://www.ama.africatoday.com). Herbstein has collected a variety of resources to help his readers that are of value to everyone. If you are looking for primary sources, the *African Times Online* site contains digital versions of this nineteenth-century newspaper (http://diva.sfsu.edu/ users/Trevor.Getz0/AfricanTimes).

If you are interested in contemporary Ghanaian issues, the Ghanaian expatriate community has developed a great site at GhanaWeb (http:// www.ghanaweb.com) for keeping in touch with issues at home and around the world.

Finally, we invite you to visit the Abina Mansah website at http://www .abina.org.

PRELIMINARY SKETCHES

THE PROBLEM OF REPRESENTATION

How do you sketch people who lived more than a century ago, and for whom we have no photographs, drawings, or other visual evidence? How can we know how Abina would have dressed when we possess no pictures of her, and the historical record includes precious few pictures of any Ghanaian women of Abina's status who lived in the last half of the nineteenth century? As the authors of this book, we shared our individual expertise areas in history and design to best approximate what Abina would have looked like and what clothes she would likely have worn, and we did the same for Melton, Davis, Brew, and Quamina Eddoo. Throughout the making of *Abina*, we debated the kind of clothes each character would have worn—the design and cut of the cloth, jewelry and other adornments, and physical features. There were countless questions for which we sought answers. We wished to ascertain whether Melton would have worn a judge's wig (he would have not), whether rural men went shirtless (yes, they did), and how common was the practice of wearing head wraps (quite common, and still so today). We pored over dozens of pictures—newspaper illustrations, missionaries' photographs, and even woodcuts—to get a feel for both the village and urban environments that would have formed Abina's world. We found that many of these sources contradicted our own assumptions as well as the typical way this period of West African history has been commonly depicted. Of course, we will never really know whether we drew Brew's suit or Abina's beads correctly, but like all historians and artists with good intentions, we based our decisions and our interpretations on the sources that were available.

ABINA MANSAH

JAMES HUTTON BREW

JAMES DAVIS

QUAMINA EDDOO

WILLIAM MELTON

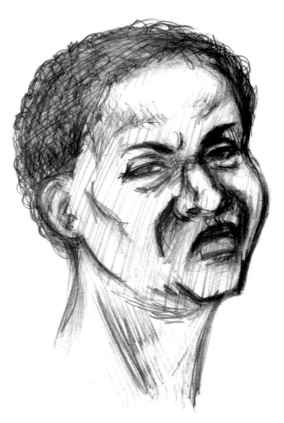

ECCOAH

KITCHEN

BAR

DAVIS' HOUSE EXTERIOR

CONSTABLE MOOSA

YAW AWOAH

TANDO

KITCHEN

MELTON'S OFFICE

BREW'S OFFICE

VILLAGE

COURTROOM

DAVIS' HOUSE
INTERIOR

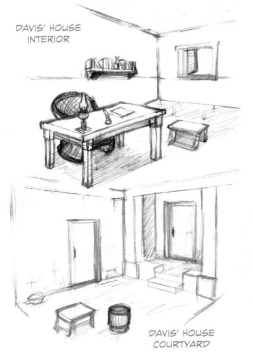

DAVIS' HOUSE
COURTYARD

NANA
AMPOFA

THOMAS
AMINISSAH

JONATHAN
DAWSON

QUAMINA EDDOO'S
HOUSE

GLOSSARY

ABUSUA *(ah-boo-sue-wa)* The matrilineal (traced through the mother) kin group that formed a core part of the identity of Akan-speaking people like Abina and Quamina Eddoo. Abusua (plural-*mmusuatow*) may have developed as early as the fourteenth century as the key support structure for individual members of society. In the nineteenth century, slaves were generally not recognized as belonging in an abusua. *(see pages 118, 120)*

ADINKRA *(ah-din-kra)* Akan ideograms, or visual symbols that convey concepts and meanings. Adinkra probably predate Arabic and Latin (English, French) script in the Gold Coast region. *(see page xix)*

AKAN *(ah-khan)* The name given to a collection of peoples speaking related languages and sharing a number of cultural institutions. The Akan make up the majority of the population of modern-day Ghana, and historically dominated a number of states including Asante and the Fante Confederation. *(see page 116)*

ASAFO *(ah-sah-foe)* Brotherhoods (and possibly sisterhoods) that have existed since at least the seventeenth century in Akan-speaking society. Membership is largely based on descent on the father's side. Asafo companies also had a paramilitary function in protecting the community from tyrannical rulers as well as outside invaders. *(see pages 118, 124–125, 152)*

ASANTE *(ah-san-tee)* The multiethnic state that emerged from Akan-speaking peoples of the West African forests in the seventeenth century. Asante went on to dominate a region roughly the size and shape of modern-day Ghana. Note that the modern pronunciation and spelling "Ashanti" is a product of sloppy British colonial spelling of the state in English, beginning as "As-hantee" but quickly becoming "Ashantee." *(see pages 118–129)*

COLONIALISM In late nineteenth-century West Africa, colonialism referred not so much to the presence of European settlers as to the imposition of formal authority or informal power by Europeans, including the British, over African peoples. Colonial rule destroyed or twisted preexisting power structures and social organizations, and replaced them with a new set of ideas and relationships that placed European values and people at the top of a social hierarchy. *(see pages 122–123, 136, 168–169)*

COLONY *(Gold Coast)* In 1876, the Gold Coast Colony was a set of small territories surrounding the major British forts and trading positions (including Cape Coast) that were formally claimed as part of the British Empire and administered directly by British administrators. *(see pages 122, 127–129)*

CONSTRUCT In the context of historical methodology, construction is the task of putting together a narrative of the past using evidence but also relying on the ideas and worldviews of the historian. *(see pages 135, 140, 150–151, 164)*

CULTURAL HISTORY A school or field of historical research that focuses on identifying and seeking to understand the perspectives of people who lived in the past rather than the causes or experiences of major events. Cultural historians rely on the method of deconstruction and tend to explore relationships between individuals and society as a whole. *(see pages 153–154)*

DECONSTRUCT In the context of historical methodology, deconstruction is the task of decoding the meanings hidden within a text or source by reading it with and against the grain. It is the search for assumptions made by the author and messages encoded in his/her writing or artistry in order to understand the ways he or she thought and possibly to reveal the worldview shared by his or her contemporaries. *(see pages 146–148, 150)*

FANTE CONFEDERATION A movement that emerged in the late 1860s to establish an African state in the region around Cape Coast modeled upon European states of the period. The Confederation's leaders were mostly formally educated men like James Hutton Brew, and they tried to tie together small states that had a long history of alliance against Asante invasion. The Confederation eventually failed when the British defeated Asante and declared a Protectorate over the region. The name is also applied to a much longer tradition of alliance among the states of the area around Cape Coast. *(see pages 120, 124, 130, 152)*

GENDER Often used as a noun to depict a static, intrinsic, binary relationship between male and female categories, this term now signals much more complex understandings of the way that societies infuse ideas about masculinity, femininity, sexuality, and identity into their political, social, and economic operations. To "gender" a study of the past means to acknowledge the role gender issues played in a society in a particular place and time and to integrate that understanding into the study design and interpretation. *(see pages 163)*

GOLD COAST This region of West Africa was named by Europeans in the sixteenth century on the basis of its population's production and sale of gold. The region, which had previously been known to at least some of its inhabitants as Wangara, was not politically unified other than briefly in the late eighteenth and early nineteenth centuries under Asante rule, and later as a British colony after 1902. *(see pages 116–122, 124–126)*

GRAPHIC HISTORY A graphic representation of the past, but also a history in that it purports to represent past events and experiences through the interpretation of sources from that period. Graphic histories are not meant to be fiction, although most authors and illustrators recognize that the narratives they are creating must at times venture into speculation. *(see pages 130–131)*

HERITAGE For our purposes, heritage is a way of thinking about the past that is different from history. Whereas history strives to be critical, heritage is generally a celebration of identity that draws upon past suffering or glories for its legitimacy. Heritage is often openly used to bring people together around a cause or identity. *(see pages 155–157)*

HISTORICIZATION The act of placing a source in the context of its time and location of origin. This process of relating a part (the source) to the whole (its historical context) is vital to deriving any accurate sense of the meaning of the source. *(see page 115)*

MATRILINEALITY A system in which ancestry is traced through the mother and maternal ancestors. *(see page 118)*

OHENE *(owe-he-nay)* The *ohene* (plural-*ahenfo*) is the ruler of an oman. In the nineteenth century, this chiefly officeholder's power was generally held in check by a network of elders, advisors, and even royal slaves. *(see pages xix, 118)*

OKYEAME *(owe-chee-ah-may)* In Akan-speaking societies, okyeame are professional linguists. They are court translators and often function as advisors or historians as well as interpreters of the law. *(see pages 152–153)*

OMAN *(owe-mahn)* An oman (plural-*aman*) is an Akan state. The term may signify a very small but independent territory such as Saltpond, but is equally applied to vast confederacies like Asante. *(see page 118)*

PATERNALISM Paternalism indicates a belief in the power and authority of the father, and it is used in the case of British relations with the Gold Coast in the nineteenth century because it was the primary way that British officials, missionaries, and others viewed their relationship with the local population. It implies both a sense of a right to dominate and a duty to discipline the locals for their own good. *(see pages 147, 168–169)*

PEOPLE WITHOUT HISTORY Another of the ways in which Europeans judged Africans. Following the evolution of a formal discipline of history in late nineteenth-century Europe, people without written documents were seen as being outside of "history" and therefore also having no claim to civilization, ownership of land, or any of the other rights of people who had "history." *(see page xv)*

PRIMARY SOURCE A document, image, oral tradition, or other record produced during or in the general period of the event or trend it is describing. *(see pages 115, 135, 201)*

PROTECTORATE *(Gold Coast)* The large southern region of modern Ghana, over which the British claimed some authority following the 1873–1874 Anglo-Asante War on the basis of agreements and alliances with local rulers. Although the British did not directly rule these territories at first, they gradually extended their legal, economic, and military power across the region. *(see page 122)*

READING AGAINST THE GRAIN This is the practice of reading a text to discover ideas and concepts inadvertently placed within it by the author. *(see page 147)*

READING WITH THE GRAIN The practice of reading a text in order to discover the author's purpose and intended message to his/her audience. *(see page 147)*

RECONSTRUCT In historical practice, the process of putting together evidence to discover "what happened" in a past time, place, and series of events. *(see pages 140, 142, 146)*

SECONDARY SOURCE Any source that is intended to be an account of an event of which the author or teller is not an eyewitness, whether oral, written, or visual. *(see page 115)*

SOCIAL HISTORY A school of history that focuses on interpreting evidence from the past to reveal the experiences of large groups of people rather than focusing on the biographies of individuals or causes of events. *(see page 153)*

WHIG Named after a British political movement, supporters of this "liberal" view of the world tend to believe that humans are making progress toward a more enlightened future, which they frame largely in middle-class, late nineteenth-century European terms. *(see page 148)*